FANTAIL

HOLD YOUR OWN HOUS

Everything you need to hold your very own house party.
How do you do it? When do you do it? Who do you do
it with? How to stop asking so many questions. It's all
here:

- Games
- Gotchas
- Gunge
- Guest Tests

And, revealed for the first time, the startling secrets
behind Noel's House Party. Crinkley Bottom – and you
– will never be the same again.

HOLD YOUR OWN
House Party

Noel Edmonds

John Machin with Dave Dutton

FANTAIL

FANTAIL BOOKS

Published by the Penguin Group
Penguin Books Ltd, 27 Wrights Lane, London w8 5TZ, England
Penguin Books USA Inc., 375 Hudson Street, New York, New York 10014, USA
Penguin Books Australia Ltd, Ringwood, Victoria, Australia
Penguin Books Canada Ltd, 10 Alcorn Avenue, Toronto, Ontario, Canada M4V 3B2
Penguin Books (NZ) Ltd, 182–190 Wairau Road, Auckland 10, New Zealand

Penguin Books Ltd, Registered Offices: Harmondsworth, Middlesex, England

First published 1994
1 3 5 7 9 10 8 6 4 2

Fantail Film and TV Tie-in edition first published 1994

Filmset by Datix International Limited, Bungay, Suffolk
Printed in England by Clays Ltd, St Ives plc
Set in 12/14 pt Monophoto Ehrhardt

Contents

Foreword

I know what you're thinking. No, apart from that. You're thinking, Noel Edmonds – bright, handsome, witty, tall, modest young chap: with such an unfair number of natural advantages, surely he can't be a silver-tongued, sophisticated house-party host as well! Well, you couldn't be wronger, Tosh.

No one has ever gone home from a Noel Edmonds house party disappointed. After stopping off at the hospital, the police station and their solicitors, they're usually far too tired for disappointment. But, as Vince, Crinkley Bottom's cinema manager, says, you can't please both of the people all of the time.

Unlike the Pitz Cinema, however, my house parties attract rather more than two Crinkley Bottom villagers – and many of them even turn up on the correct night. Thus, over the years, I've acquired an experience of house parties unparalleled throughout the length and breadth of Crinkleyshire – a county, keen Bottomists will be interested to learn, which is now so small, its breadth is actually longer than its length.

In addition to my own expertise, I have been able to draw on the help of Edmondses old and new. Through personal memories, the services of Crinkley Bottom's small medium Pygmy Rose Lee, and a cheap-day return to Wormwood Scrubs, the wisdom of the Edmonds dynasty has been garnered, sifted and laid down like a bucket of fine Crinkley Bottom wine within these pages.

Great-Aunt Flo, Cousin Quasimodo, Uncle Cornelius, Great-Grandfather Svengali, Dame Lucrezia, Great-Niece Vanity and Peaches have all contributed. But special mention must be made of Great-Uncle Ebeneezer at whose ankle I learned so much – and for a surprisingly small fee. Great-Uncle Eb was such a considerate host – he insisted on seeing each of his house party guests home personally. Some nights he was gone for weeks. A fine man, now sadly no longer with us, although we're expecting him back some time next October.

This, then, is the remarkable pedigree of the magnum opus you hold before you. All that remains is for you to turn its crisp, Crinkley first page, and embark on a starry-eyed voyage of discovery through a twinkling universe of tips, advice, knowledge and know-how. Oh, and just pop across to the counter and pay for it first, eh? People are beginning to think you're a display stand.

The Great House, February 1994

1. How to be Noel

How to be me? Who at one time has not asked him or herself that question? Well, yes, maybe Raquel Welch. And the Emperor of Japan. And Mel Gibson. And Frank Bruno, Rupert Murdoch, Pavarotti, Andrew Lloyd Webber, and any one of the multi-millions of people who died before I was born, yes. OK, so it was a rhetorical question, the sort that doesn't expect a proper answer. A bit like those you get on your tax-return form.

What I was trying to say was: who hasn't wondered what it takes to be the perfect house party host? Funny you should ask, because people watch me at my house parties, and think, sheesh! if he can do it, must be a piece of cake. Let me tell you, it's not a piece of anything. It's traumatic.

Oh yes, I smile a lot, look cheerful, force myself to have the odd drink. I even occasionally dive into the fish pond from the Great House balcony in polka-dot jodhpurs with a plastic lampshade on my head. But I'm not enjoying myself. Acting, you see. Deep down, below this suave exterior, I'm anxious, I'm apprehensive, I'm constantly on the alert.

No, it's not Cook's prune and fig pie. I'm all of these things because – look, this might shock you, so I'd advise sensitive readers (yes, both of you) to sit down at this point; if necessary, put the book back on the shelf and ask the cashier for a chair. I'm all of these things because that is what it takes to be the perfect house party host. And you thought it was just a question of laying on some authentic Crinkley Bottom vol-au-vents, and standing behind the non-drivers when they fall over.

That's part of it, yes. A rather large part if you've a high percentage of journalists on your guest list. But there are so many other aspects to being the perfect host, it's impossible ever to relax. Taut as Elizabeth Taylor's forehead, me.

A saying I learned at Great-Uncle Ebeneezer Edmonds's ankle has it that a host should be, as the title suggests, Hospitable, Observant, Sympathetic and Teetotal. I'm not wholly in agreement with this view. Nor do I agree with Multi-Great-Grandma Lucrezia who stated that host is short for hostility.

To my mind, the perfect house party host is part best friend, part nanny, with a smattering of Dutch uncle, sugar daddy, marriage guidance counsellor, compère, toastmaster, spouse, fiancé, flirt, fashion model, nurse, chemist, etiquette coach, mechanic, priest, psychiatrist, Samaritan, ambassador, referee, philosopher, army general, archaeologist, matador, Santa Claus, kick boxer and camel herder. No, I'm being silly. You don't have to be a nanny at all. Nonetheless, you begin to appreciate the size of the task before you.

Don't despair yet, though – plenty of time for that when the bills arrive – for there is a way to target certain key issues in order to turn you instantly into the perfect house party host. Unfortunately I don't know what it is, but if you come across it, let me know; it'll save us both an enormous amount of time. Meanwhile, I'll convey in my own way the vast wealth of hostly savoir-faire I've accumulated from countless house parties over many years.

First, clothes. You're going to need some. I have several natty little outfits (well, not that little) – favourite among them a snazzy number comprising trousers in chewing-gum grey, jacket in eyepatch pink, shirt in pigeon-dropping white, shoes in lorry-rollerdoor brown, tie in Arctic-explorer blue, socks in Scottish-goalkeeper's-face red, and waistcoat in motorway-service-station-food black. The Wool Shop's Prudence Prendergast, known locally as the woman who puts the bull into ensemble, describes the effect as two dozen parrots squashed on a stained-glass window. Fine. I'm glad she likes it.

Smartness, you see; that's the ticket with clothes. Tatty jacket, frayed jeans, baggy sweatshirt, holy socks and a pair of cheap pumps may be your idea of the perfect hostly clobber: but it's improper and unseemly, and you simply won't get away with it. And don't think I haven't tried.

A quality the perfect host also needs is the ability to deal with people in a tactful, sensitive, considerate and charming manner. So that rules out most Crinkley Bottomers! The Edmonds family, on the other hand, are noted for their careful handling of guests. Cousin Peaches, however, was noted for his careful guesting of handles. But that's another story.

Luckily, this talent seems to be hereditary. When

house party violence looms, you won't find me running around waving my arms about like an idiot. In fact, you won't find me at all. I always have a couple of big bouncers on hand. Oh, please, come on now.

As I said, I pay – rather, employ – two large bouncers, Tug and Crusher Nuttz, to sort out any unpleasantness – arguments, fights, gatecrashers, Tony Blackburn. They're lethal lads: thick, solid shoulders, and heads to match; the sort who never use two words when a smack in the mouth will do. As posh Great-Aunt Felicity Edmonds used to say, 'What's the point of keeping a hound and kicking yourself up the jacksey?'

Sadly, there will be times when direct contact with the more fearsome side of house parties is unavoidable, and I'm not talking about Cook's prune and fig pie here either. There exists in this world a seditious network of so-called people, dedicated to undermining the house party we all know and love. Albeit brooding, menaceful and vengeful within, outwardly they appear ordinary and unexceptional; practically indistinguishable from normal people like you and me. In fact, the only way to recognize them is by their hands. At house parties, they'll usually be around your throat. I'm referring to – take a deep breath – the neighbours.

I would have nothing whatsoever against neighbours, if only they didn't live next door! As it is, every time you hold the merest mega-celebration, they just go to pieces. Or, occasionally, PCs. Oh yes, even we've had the police round at the Great House. 1950, I think it was. Or maybe it was nearer nine o'clock. Some piffling complaint from that old chap down the lane with the phobia fetish.

Rang and told them our music was too loud. I ask you! Wasting police time on something so blatantly petty, trivial, and untrue. I wouldn't have minded, but we'd already offered to replace the roof that had vibrated off his bungalow.

Like any perfect house party host, I was happily *au fait* with the procedure for dealing effectively with officers of the law; that is, writing down your own entirely honest account of the incident, and handing it to them stapled to a £20 note. Yes, the loss of money is a little upsetting, but with 16 weeks in bed and a course of intensive grief counselling, you'll be as right as rain!

Now where were we up to? Oh, yes: our eyes in neighbours. The acid test of a perfect host comes when you're confronted by that special breed of neighbour who circumvents legal alleyways and storms around to complain in person and plaid dressing-gown. These aren't your ordinary, common-or-gardening neighbours. These are huge, bristle-chinned, balloon-bicepped, mobile monoliths. Muscles on their DNA. And the male version's even worse. 500,000 years' more evolution and at 100 yards they might just be mistaken for the missing link.

Technically speaking, such neighbours are hunter-gatherers: they hunt you down, and gather your shirt front in their fists. There's absolutely no point arguing with them; very few of them have mastered the art of language yet.

So, how do you deal with these creatures? How do I as the perfect host handle the irate primate with his hand around my thorax? No, I don't kick him anywhere.

Physical violence is not the answer. The Edmonds family has never considered that maxim about fighting fire with fire a particularly sensible idea. You'd be really chuffed to see the fire brigade roll up at your blazing homestead with two dozen bunsen burners and a flamethrower, wouldn't you?

No, the perfect house party host never ever contemplates for the merest hint of a moment perpetrating violence upon the person of any other human being on the surface of the planet. Unless he happens to be smaller than you, of course. Nor should you ever hit a man with glasses. Draw up a table, and offer to help him empty them, instead. Reasoning with him's no good. In fact, the only sane approach is rank, unadulterated cowardice. I'm not talking here about that sneaky, subtle cowardice most grown-ups go in for: I mean the real thing.

Cowardice gets a bad press. Why, I've never dared to ask. But it's puzzling; heroism is nothing but a primitive reflex action: you see a pair of hoodlums beating up a helpless, defenceless person like you or me – well, you – and you plough in unthinkingly to rescue him.

Cowardice calls for altogether more sophisticated abilities: the ability to stop and assess the risks; the ability to disregard other people's opinions of you; the ability to bunk off like a baboon with its bottom on fire. As Great-Uncle Ebeneezer once said, 'Any fool can be an idiot: cowardice takes real courage.'

The type of courageous cowardice needed in the case of this neighbour who's now gripping five-thirds of your body in his eyebrows lies in employing the only

remaining part of you capable of movement – no, your
vocal cords – in a brave and forthright display of pathetic
pleading.

In Crinkley Bottom, the Edmondses are well-known
little pleaders, and their collected cowardly pleas have
been stored for centuries in the Great House library,
behind the settee. Some of the greatest are reproduced
here in the hope that they may assist in your bid to
become the perfect host by helping you avoid house
party fisticuffs. If they don't work, wear a black armband;
it'll match your eye.

'Pain has an unfortunate tendency to hurt me.'
'I'm sure you could think of something better to do
    with your hands – like comb them.'
'I am the American Secretary of State for Defence,
    and you are under covert surveillance by 200 armed
    agents of the CIA. Go away.'
'I refuse to hit a man who's not wearing glasses.'
'I never fight on the anniversary of the death of my
    Great-Aunt's best friend's personal chiropodist's whist
    partner's hamster.'
'Promise you'll let me nibble your ear in the clinches.'
'Here's five thousand pounds.'

Having survived your close encounter of the neighbourly
kind, and undergone the major surgery necessary to
repair your ego, you, the perfect host, still cannot relax.
While all about you guests are beginning to make sloshing
noises as they move, and sausage rolls are being tested
for their aerodynamic capabilities, you must remain aloof

7

and sensible in order to be that most important of perfect hostly traits – romantic. Sorry. It's in the rules.

For people like me, romance is like a randy dog: it comes to us naturally. Others have to work at it. If you're among the latter category – and you are, believe me – you're going to need a few tips, namely:

1. **Change your socks:** If you're hoping to sweep your house party guests off their feet in a whirlwind of romantic fervour, the condition of your socks is unlikely to be uppermost in your mind. But this is no excuse for wearing the same pair until they smell like dead fish and become glued to your feet with baked sweat. Even fresh socks leave a lot to be desired – especially the polyester purple ones with dayglow lemon lightning flashes, and measle spots on the ankles. If you must wear socks, at least try to buy something discreet, change them regularly and often, and see if you can remember to wash them occasionally before you put them back on. You want guests to fall at your feet, not faint on them.

2. **Write poetry:** Romantic with a capital aargh, this. Not everyone can write poetry, though. You have to have a pen. And not just any old pen. It's got to have ink in it. Mauve, preferably; although pink, crocus, aquamarine, cobalt, grey and plum are also permissible, depending on your mood. This may change with the seasons, but should always appear deeply preoccupied with thoughts of rabbits.

Only when you have acquired pen, ink, mood and wastepaper basket can you begin to poem. And this is where the danger lies. As with most romantic gambits, writing poetry is just the limp end of the wedge. It might start with a few lines of harmless rhyming verse. But then, suddenly, you've got a sonnet. Soon, you're sliding down the slippery slope to alliteration. And before you know it, you've grown a beard, moved to Grasmere, and started wandering lonely as a cloud looking for golden blooming daffodils. This may seem like a desirable method of obtaining a romantic aura to some people, but most sane, red-blooded hosts prefer a far more difficult and challenging solution. Like changing their socks.

3. **Be a millionaire**: Millionaires excite the guests' hormones faster than stirring their thyroids with a ladle. And it's not hard to be one; most millionaires find the life pretty easy, in fact. Unfortunately, where romanticness is concerned, it's not sufficient just to be a millionaire: you have to be seen to be one. This can be achieved in various tasteful ways – and, surprisingly, having the words 'I AM A MILLIONAIRE' tattooed across your forehead in luminous orange paint is not one of them. You can, for example, secretly donate a well-publicized sum to charity, light your cigars with £50 notes, buy incredibly expensive works of art for the nation, or eat on British Rail. The snag is, by the time you've done all that, you'll be broke and no longer a romantic millionaire. But all's not lost; house party guests will still associate with the wretchedly poor host. Provided they're assured a change of identity and a new life in South America afterwards, of course.

4. **Whisper in people's ears**: The romantic art of

ear-whispering requires a certain degree of intimacy: with female guests, you need to know them pretty well before you can even find their ears. But it's worth hunting round until you're sure. Mistakes can be embarrassing.

5. **Open doors:** The key to successful door-opening is in the wrist action. A smooth, measured twist on the handle can make even strong guests squeak with delight. Combine this with determined manly pulling power, nimble footwork and a flamboyant directional sweep of the non-opening arm, and they'll practically melt beneath your romantic hostly charm.

Timing's important, too. Open your door too eagerly, and you can be hanging around for days waiting for someone to walk through. Open it too late, and you'll break their nose – which may seem wonderfully amusing at the time; but you won't be laughing when you get a bill from their plastic surgeon.

6. **Be strong and silent:** Throughout history, guests of all ages have been romantically drawn towards the strong, silent host. It's probably something to do with the theory that opposites attract. Being strong and silent requires a certain amount of sacrifice and self-control. And it helps if you can be tall, dark and handsome, too. So I'm told. Otherwise, it's simply a matter of having a throbbing body, exuding immense power, and maintaining a refined, persistent silence. But try to take a break from it now and then, or guests will think you're a Rolls Royce.

7. **Arch one eyebrow:** If you're concerned about the ratio of energy expended to the benefits received, you'll

find arching one eyebrow is by far the most economical way of being romantic, and it certainly beats the heck out of changing your socks. Why female guests in particular find this romantic is a mystery. Eyebrow-arching itself is just one of many secondary physiological feats, like ear-wiggling, knuckle-cracking and belching at will. But try bewitching them with one of these, and the only bed you'll end up in will have NHS pillows and frowns round the side.

8. **Be breathless:** This is easily the most straightforward method of demonstrating your latent romantic proclivities. And, for once, there's such a huge, rich and rewarding variety of examples to choose from: asthma, anaemia, anxiety, acute shock, bronchitis, croup, pneumonia . . . Takes your breath away, doesn't it?

9. **Be French:** Frenchmen are massively romantic. The way they make donkey noises down their noses, the way they eat snails and smell of garlic, the way they wear berets and hate the English. Brontosaurusly romantic! In fact, they're so flaming romantic, they're the envy of all Europe. No wonder the poor twits keep getting invaded.

To be romantic, it's not necessary to copy everything the French do – fortunately, because it's not legal to copy everything the French do. The perfect host finds it sufficient merely to pack his nose with garlic and spatter his house party conversation with a little Gaul talk, such as:

Malade: A sick duck.
Faux pas: The father of my enemy.

Après: After the church service.

Après moi, le déluge: Kindly wait until there's more room at the urinal.

Entente cordiale: A drink in a marquee.

Oeuf: A horse's foot.

Appeler: To call for an apple.

Haute cuisine: Making porridge.

Jamais: Covered in marmalade.

Après ski: I've eaten my yoghurt.

Tour de force: A walk round the police station.

Coiffeur: Heavy drinker.

Par excellence: A good round of golf.

Neuf: A new smell.

Maître d'hôtel: Table salesman.

Toulouse: Twin lavatories.

Exposé: (pronounced ex-pozay) A dead bunch of flowers.

Seine: The second longest river in France (pronounced sane. In fact, probably the only thing in France that can be pronounced sane).

I'm indebted, to the tune of £5 – five pounds! – for the foregoing helpful translations to Great-Niece Vanity Edmonds. Vanity, named after every member of the family, picked up the lingo with typical Edmonds aplomb when she went on a birthday train trip to the French capital last summer. It was a wonderful surprise; her mother had actually asked for a day return to Powys.

Romanticness, however, be it of the French, strong-silent, or clean-socked variety, breaks no ice at house parties when it comes to handling VIPs, or Very

Impotent Persons, as they're known by the end of the evening.

VIPs tend to be a solitary lot; they like to be introduced to the nearest bottle, and left to get on with it. The perfect host, therefore, does just that: he plants them in a quiet, well-stocked corner, with a funnel and a spare liver. He does not take advantage of his position to prevail upon VIPs for autographs. This is sycophantic, infra-dig and usually impractical, as the big-headed, obnoxious ones can't even write propallee.

By now, half of you will be thinking that there's a deal more to being me than meets the magnifying-glass. The other half will be thinking they'd better get a move on if they're going to finish this book before the shop shuts.

You're both right, because, like the Great House chamberpot-maid after one of Cook's prune and fig pie dinners, big jobs lie ahead of you. Indeed, for perfect host aspirants, the story's only just beginning. Having mastered the principal arts already mentioned, you now have to acquire the many other characteristics which pepper your path to perfection like skidmarks on the way to the Liszt and Newt.

Uppermost among them is decisiveness, possibly. And I don't care what anyone says, you also have to be open-minded. Next, as I was saying only yesterday to the Reverend Dews in the mixed sauna, you must be discreet. Then there's fortitude, equanimity, urbanity, dignity, elegance, consideration, empathy, dedication, alertness, tolerance, optimism – and brevity.

Oh, and you have to have a er, what do you call it? . . . good memory; and be dead refined, and lively – even if it kills you, and non-repetitive, and unambiguous-ish, and non-repetitive, and modest – like me, and sincere – whether you mean it or not, and uncondescending – obviously. And finally, you have to be humble, which is something I find particularly easy.

And that, as the short-stocked auctioneer said of his sale catalogue, is about the lot. Except for another final thing: servants. No matter how perfect he is himself, the perfect party host knows his choice of servants can mean the difference between success and failure. So my advice is: get them young – while they still know everything.

(Courses on How to be Noel are currently being held at the Great House every Thursday. Interested parties are advised to arrive by seven p.m. and bring a box.)

PERFECT HOST HICCUPS!

Noel's Top 15 Excuses for Being Caught Drunk in Charge of a House Party

'I've been commissioned by a national newspaper to check on how the police deal with drunk and disorderly suspects.'

'The chap in the shop swore it was non-alcoholic whisky.'

'Staff birthday: I've been toasting the chambermaid centuplets.'

'I've just got this thing against kidneys.'

'I haven't dropped a touch.'

'I'm doing it to save the youth of this country from temptation – the more I drink, the less there'll be for them.'

'The hangover pills are nearly past their sell-by date.'

'I breathed in too deeply near Maurice Chinking-Jacket.*'

'Nobody's having *my* liver after I'm dead.'

'You're all so beautiful I wanted to see two of you.'

'I'm not drunk: I always wear my trousers on my head on Saturdays.'

'I was pouring a crate of old lager down the drain, and I just sort of – missed.'

'I never touched a drop until I was sixteen; I'm making up for lost time.'

'I've got a bottle of scotch in my inside pocket: it's osmosis.'

'I'm not drunk: you're just more sober than usual.'

*Crinkley Bottom's freelance journalist.

2. The Guest Test

Now you know how to be Noel and therefore the perfect house party host, you have to decide who to invite. That's not so easy, when there are always people around to spoil even the best house party – they're called guests. So what you need is this guest test – a psychologically revealing questionnaire to send to invitees in order to judge their suitability for your house party.

If you were going to one of Noel's house parties, would you take –
a) a bottle?
b) an Upper Class Twit-to-English phrase book?
c) a week off from eating?
d) an overdose?
e) a mat to kneel on while chatting to your host?

Should house party introductions be made by –
a) the host?
b) the buffet table?
c) 8.25 p.m.?
d) pointing one guest at another and telling them to get on with it?
e) a self-defence expert with a working knowledge of the law on slander?

The 'Quarter-of-an-Hour Guffaw': Thirty seconds laughing, fourteen and a half minutes looking around for your teeth

Is the correct method of laughing at a house party to –

a) emit a burst of tiny machine-gun fire from the top of your nostrils?

b) attempt to transpose your ears and shoulders five times in succession while saying, 'Orf, orf, orf'?

c) implant the back of your head between your shoulder blades, and imagine you're in the process of trying to swallow a chandelier?

d) appear to make several determined bids to draw a particularly reluctant chunk of nasal debris into the upper reaches of your cranium?

THNAT
THNAT

THNIT
THNIT

The 'Hiawatha Chortle': Climaxes in a mini-haha

e) crouch forward, pound your knees, whoop hysterically,
  and ask someone to send for an osteopath?

**At the house parties you attend, do you call the
butler –**
a) der, um, er, em, eh, erm, uh – you there?
b) Sweetie?
c) while jumping up and down and waving an empty
  glass above your head in a life and death fashion?
d) Dad?

The 'Minus-Five-Degrees-Celsius Bellow': It's a little roar

e) when your blood-alcohol ratio is in danger of falling
   below 1:1?

**You are at a house party when the host comes over
and asks if you'd care to try your hand on his
organ. Do you –**
a) suspect someone's been talking?
b) pretend you didn't hear and ask him to pass the nuts?
c) think he's mistaken you for a virtuoso?
d) blush demurely and politely but firmly decline?
e) blush demurely and politely but firmly punch him in
   the mouth?

The 'Shingles Chuckle': Rough, infectious, and it gets on your nerves

If a house party waiter gave you a hors d'oeuvre, would you –
a) prune it?
b) pump it?
c) ask him if he knows where you can get some string for it?
d) jump away quickly and rub your arm with goosegrease?

e) see your doctor immediately?

At Noel's house party dinners, would you expect the cheese to be passed –
a) from left to right?
b) its best?
c) so quickly you barely have a chance to sniff it?
d) back and forth until the dog comes within feeding range?
e) by the British Food Standards Authority in a moment of complete insanity?

Your elbow is nudged at a house party, causing the olive in your drink to plop out into the cleavage of the lady you're speaking to. Do you –
a) pretend not to notice?
b) offer to get it out?
c) offer to get the olive out?
d) lock all the doors, summon the waiter and demand another olive?
e) think you've seen the film, with Barbara Windsor in it?

To make a good impression at a house party, should you talk about –
a) the disgraceful lack of parking spaces for your helicopters?
b) the Queen – or Liz, as she insists you call her?
c) Noel Edmonds – and how you've never heard of him?
d) the nuisance of having to fly to Zurich to complain about your bank charges?
e) once?

You are dining at a house party when the guest
alongside you places a hand on your knee. Should
you –
a) shake it?
b) ask the butler to remove it?
c) be grateful?
d) apologize for being born with your knee in such an
   awkward place?
e) stab it with the hand-on-your-knee knife?

Do you consider it time to leave a house party
when you see your host's –
a) eyelids begin to droop?
b) pyjamas being brought down to him?
c) sawn-off shot-gun pointing at your forehead?
d) bouncing new baby boy leaving for work?
e) skeleton beginning to show through?

How did they score?

(a) 20, (b) 1, (c) 0, (d) 5, (e) 10

0–1: Ask this chap to pass the port, and he'd give you a
photograph of Grimsby. He thinks petits-fours are
slightly dangerous golf strokes; his idea of evening dress
is pyjamas; and the only vintage wine he's experienced is
in the wheel bearing of his 1966 Ford Cortina. In short,
he's crass and vulgar and what he knows about house
parties could be written on the back of a hermit's
Christmas card list. Invite him; he'll make it seem as if
you know what you're doing.

2–3: Ah, yes, the Crinkley Bottom villager type; a really handy chap to have at house parties: sound, solid, tough, reliable, honest as the Crinkley Bottom tea break is long. You must invite him – not as a guest; you can use him as a coat rack.

4–5: This is the classic life and know-all of the party: A-level in taking exams; able to quote all four TV weather forecasts verbatim, and still can't get it right; reads newspapers from the front; always has the last word on everything from the badger's lavatorial habits to the price of mung beans on the Burkina-Faso stock exchange. No point asking him to fill in a questionnaire; he'll already know whether he should come or not.

6–10: If you're intending to invite this twit to your house party, it's only fair to point out to him that a canapé is not something that keeps the sun off you. As anyone who's been to my garden parties knows, that role is more than adequately taken care of by the British weather.

11–20: A bit iffy, this one – underpant shirt tucker; spider collection; holidays in Rhyl; two duffel coats, one for best; Radio 2 sticker on his table-tennis bat bag; allowed into discothèques without being frisked. Very borderline. Better invite him, though. You've got to have something for the goldfish to watch.

21–30: No doubt about this one; it's a journalist, a member of that indomitable breed of seekers after the truth: fearless, dignified, discerning, honourable. Invite him, but hide the scotch.

31–40: This person is single-minded, forthright, ambitious, decisive – almost certainly a Member of Parliament. Whoaa! don't set fire to their invitation. It's important to have politicians at your house party. Quite apart from the glorious system of democratic government they represent, it gives the servants someone to look down on.

41–50: Early twenties, highly amusing, at a peak – and that's just his IQ. Invite him; he could become a top TV presenter.

51–60: This person is to house party gatherings what the veterinary glove is to cows. He's vindictive, malicious, evil, unscrupulous, sly, despicable and, to be frank, not very nice. In fact, he thinks a favour is an upper-class £5 note, and his idea of a good turn is a well-behaved seagull. Invite him, anyway. Who knows – he might ask you to his parents' wedding.

61–70: This lady is as tasteless as last February's chewing-gum – and even harder to remove from under your dinner table. She arrives late, about fifteen minutes after her eyelashes. She's been held up at Monsieur Paulo's Hair and Beauty Salon – waiting for a refund. Her hat's quite pleasant, although the corks don't really match; and her heels are so high, half a dozen guests get seasick just watching her walk in. Nonetheless, this person is a welcome addition to your guest list and can liven up the house party no end. Just don't let anyone use the chrome spiral staircases she always seems to stand between. They're her earrings.

71–80: This is more like it. What a splendid young lady

– vibrant, attractive, daring, fresh, friendly, fun-loving. Forget the invitation; ask her what's she's doing next Friday night.

81–100: Meticulous, punctilious, conscientious: what we've got here is an accountant. Don't tut! They're not all boring. I can remember the Great House Party of '75 – quite a feat, as I was barely into my teens at the time, of course. Most likely village guests were in the local hospital's shock unit recovering from a Crinkley Bottom Wonderers home win, so we took a chance and invited the Crinkley Bottom accountant, Adam Upfast. Reputedly, he would have bored everyone into a coma at fifty paces, but I recall taking the chap over a glass of my punch and a crash helmet, and he recounted a fascinating tale of how he was once balancing the books of a local company, using the double-entry system, when the head of the bought-ledger department unearthed three outstanding pro-forma invoices bearing incorrect VAT registration numbers, which had been correlated with the counterfoils of an order docket and . . . . . .
. . . . . . Oh, sorry. Must have dropped off there for a moment. Where was I? Ah, yes – accountants: boring gits. Don't let them within twenty miles of your house party.

101–120: Ideally, you should think twice before inviting this person as a guest. But I don't suppose you've got a month to spare.

121–140: You know the stereotypical dream girl: sleek and sensuous with ripe strawberry lips, butter-smooth skin, quicksand eyes, legs longer than an NHS waiting list, and hair frolicking behind her like a young afghan hound? Well, this is her friend.

141–160: If you're hoping for a successful house party, give this chap a miss. Or, if you're feeling really cruel, give him a Mrs.

161–180: Sit down, take a deep breath. Calm? OK, this is the score of an estate agent. No, come back! And put that crucifix down. Admittedly, estate agents are to house parties what pigeons are to windscreens. But this chap is most likely just another human being, struggling to make a living as best he can. It's wrong to discount him purely on the basis of what's probably just an outmoded, stereotypical piece of blinkered prejudice. As a civilized, open-minded member of society, it's nothing short of your duty to invite him. You don't have to be a damn fool and give him your address, though, do you?

181–200: Ah, *l'élite*! A connoisseur of fine food. A guru of good wine. An aficionado of intelligent conversation. A true aristocrat of all that's excellent about the elegant, exquisite, upper-class British house party. Save yer stamp.

201–220: Oh, dear. We've got a right one here. He thinks manners are big country houses, and his idea of the social graces is picking his nose with a knife and fork. He's tactless, uncouth, vain, and embarrassing. You definitely don't want to invite someone like this to your house party. Shame, really, because I'd have liked to have come.

221–240: Mirroring your very own standards, interests and inclinations, you'll find this chap a priority choice for your house party invitation. Get him to apply for parole immediately.

3. Who to Invite

Noel's List of Recommended Crinkley Bottom Guests

Adam Upfast (*accountant*)
Robin M. Rotten (*solicitor*)
Basher Kickett (*TV repairman*)
Horace Peebey (*bird protectionist*)
Thicky Nobwit (*trainee village idiot*)
Chippy Descartes (*existential carpenter*)

Thicky Nobwit: Needs to be introduced to himself on arrival

The Frizzetts: The only twins not to have been born in chronological order

Ronnie and Reggie Chair (*professional defendants*)
Larry Gary Harry Barry-Parry (*vegetarian abattoir manager*)
The three Frizzett twins (*of Diane Frizzett, ex-Lunatic Fringe Hair Salon*)
Tommy 'Jug-Handles' Squirter (*hero of the Great Coathanger Shortage*)
Rita Slaghips (*sumo golfer*)
Prudence Prendergast (*village wool magnate*)
Nobby Magnusson (*railway porter spotter*)
Phil E. Buster (*grease investigator and tea-money fan*)
Gordon Bennett-Moore-Guff (*puncture repair kit repairman*)
I. B. Fuddled (*sock adviser*)

Squinty Travis (*international rice artist and cushion planner*)
Bill Follows (*founder member of Crinkley Bottom Loners' Club*)
Snooty Somerville (*Sellotape sniffer*)
Herbert Bullsitter (*Council leader and spelling mistake*)
Me

4. Who Probably Not to Invite

Pru's List of Recommended Crinkley Bottom Guests

Elsie Dee (*digital watch maker*)
Anne Finely (*CBTV newsreader*)
How Jufeel (*CBTV interviewer*)
Hugh Dunnett (*village detective*)
Miss Ann Thrope (*village recluse*)
Gipsy Woes Lee (*lisping misfortune teller*)
Jaws Bush (*part-time workaholic*)
Mr Briggs (*long-term unemployed brain surgeon*)
Mr Long (*Crinkley Bottom's Best Dressed Man, and naturist*)
Mrs Bulstrode (*Pea Shoppe empress and county impersonator*)
The Reverend Dews (*vicar and Paranoid Club pencil-top taster*)
Lady Phillippa Yoyo-Bloomers (*font skinny-dipping suspect*)
Maurice Chinking-Jacket (*journalist and human drinks trolley*)
Specky Liverspot (*beauty parlour refund millionairess*)
Derek Jung (*Dangley End philosopher and cult plumber*)
Tosh Scrivener (*graduate in Illegal Parties at Crinkleyshire University*)

Clodaugh Bumpin-Melons and the Reverend Dews (the Reverend's the one with the spectacles)

Daph Titted (*Crinkley Bottom Radio's subtitling manager*)
Clodaugh Bumpin-Melons (*fruit model and gelding breeder's assistant*)

Lanky Chegwin (*moth boy*)
Tiny Blackburn (*Fishmonger of the Year and mint owner*)
Noel Edmonds (*grasshopper's knee expert*)

5. What to Wear

Woolly Advice from Pru on what to wear come the big day

Oh! Hello, are you there? This is Prudence Prendergast, proprietress of Crinkley Bottom's Wool Shop, reporting for Noel Edmonds on the subject of what to wear at a house party.

For you gentlemen, I can't offer any better advice than to look at Noel. Study him, note his dress sense, check the quality of the material: the cut, the style, the texture. And try to dress as differently from him as possible. Ooh, dear! I do hope nobody's reading this to him. Sorry, Noel, if they are. Yah boo, Shorty, if they're not.

Well, it's not fair. Here am I, proprietressing the finest wool shop this side of Firker's Wood, a woman whose frontage is admired from here to Bumpkin's End – that's the shop's frontage, riff-raff – and the local gentlemen on offer have about as much sartorial imagination as an Eskimo's cobbler. Do Eskimos have cobblers? All that deep snow and freezing temperatures, you'd think – whoops! Stop it, Pru.

Now, where was I? Oh, yes. Little wonder I'm still a spinster. Walk down the aisle with any of the fellows from Crinkley Bottom, people'd think you're collecting a penny for the guy. I'm not casting dispersions here – hurling a few, maybe. But not at little Noelie. Noel has problems peculiar to himself. Very peculiar. For one thing, he simply can't wear enough colours to match his hair. Then there's that 90-inch waist: 32-inch stomach, 58-inch money belt.

So it's no exaggeration to say that the only style in Crinkley Bottom is in the hedge around Muckflirter's Meadow. There's nothing wrong with a house party guest dressing to show off his best feature, but when you get Baggy Schofield turning up in see-through socks and a wart pouch, well honestly!

Ooh, I hope you don't think I'm being snooty about this. I'm really ever so tolerant when it comes to gentlemen's clothes. They can wear them or leave them off completely for my money (that's £75, if anyone out there's interested in taking me up). But I do like to see a man smartly turned out at a house party – and at Noel's house parties, most of the men should be smartly turned out.

It's frightfully depressing for someone with taste like what I've got. No names, no libel writs, but if you're going to wear a donkey jacket to a house party, at least remove the donkey's ears first. And those tourniquet-tight trousers under-butler Bunion feels he has to wear: talk about leaving with the after-dinner mince.

Possibly the only item of gent's clothing I've approved of at Noel's house parties was Lord Nose's waxed jacket. At least, it was until I found out he'd developed a nasty ear infection.

It's not as if there's anything hard in gentlemen's clothes. Correct house party attire is just a question of dressing sensibly. And that, Pigmy Hislop, does not

Busy guests are not advised to emulate this costume worn by four villagers to a 1923 house party. It took them thirty-six hours to turn round before going home

mean pinning two dozen little mints around the top of your jersey, and calling it a polo-neck sweater. Nor, Sniffer Dimbleby, does it mean wearing a polka-dot tie to dinner so no one will notice if you splash your soup.

Next to Fanny Smalls, the most common thing at Noel's house parties is flannel. This would be eminently acceptable, if only it was part of the gents' clothing, rather than their conversation. It's disgraceful. Crinkley Bottom men simply have no idea how to make the least worst of themselves.

There's a lot to be said for reticence, but there are occasions when you have to put your foot down, take the bull by the horns, throw down the gauntlet, and say something. Even if it's only sorry. What am I talking about, you ask? And you're not the first. I often ask myself the same question. I'm talking about certain gentlemen at Noel's house parties wearing Victorian costume – spats, ruffs, monocles, capes, bowlers, frothy cuffs, frock-coats. It's really not on, you know. Crinkley Bottom's a nice village; we don't want it spoilt by any of this modern nonsense.

Another house party fashion you'd do well to ignore is 'Pocketmania', the habit of Crinkley Bottom gentlemen to rabbit-warren their garments with special pockets for all possible, and many impossible, contingencies.

I'd rather not single anyone out for criticism. But I'm going to. Willie Touchett, Crinkley Bottom Wonderers' ballaphobic soccer star, generally turns up in a rain-hooded vest and sawn-off crombie, sporting no fewer than sixty-six pockets – purse pocket, car key pocket, tank rivet pocket, friendly ferret pocket, nose-picking knife pocket, emergency parachute pocket, secret pocket, not particularly secret but wouldn't want my mum looking in here pocket, someone else's windscreen wiper pocket, extremely serious pocket, *Noel's Official Guide to Crinkley Bottom* book pocket, pocket pocket, squashed daddy-long-legs recovery pocket, automatic washing machine spares (1973–5) pocket, nostril hair flame gun pocket, amusingly shaped eel pocket, gnat butter pocket, modelled tripe pocket, promising conker pocket, mauve rabbit dye pocket, home lunacy testing kit pocket, banana brush and comb set pocket, unidentified grey button pocket, bits of gold-filled teeth from the Liszt and Newt snug floor pocket, stand-by plankton pocket. If he lies down after dinner, twenty-two men could have a game of snooker on him.

That's about as far as I'm going to delve into gentlemen's clothes now, although someone might get lucky at Noel's next – whoops! Pru! I don't know what's coming over you. Sorry. I should never have agreed to do this on Noel's typewriter; I don't care if he did reduce the hire charge specially.

Brighter readers will already have discerned that I'm not one to criticize, but at Noel's house parties, only the servants are fetching. Clodaugh Bumpin-Melons singularly doesn't need any pointers, but the rest haven't got a clue. Don't take my word for it. Let me give you some examples from a typical house party up at the Great House.

First, there's local councillor, Penelope Utter-Twaddle. She's always dressed to kill – a bear, by the look of it. Then you've got Lurgy Ogden's cockney sister, Kaff – a woman so worried about upsetting the neighbours, she listens to her radio with the sound off. Kaff always turns up at house parties looking like a million dollars – looking like a million dollars have been stuffed down her bloomers in loose change, that is.

Next, there's cook of the Crinkley Café and active member of the Save the Salmonella Bacteria Society, Marge Rean. It's said that you can tell a great deal about people from their clothes. In Marge's case, if she's only wearing one stocking, you can tell she's made steamed pudding for tea again.

My old friend – very! old friend – Mrs Bulstrode is a

Producing this 1916 Crinkley Bottom creation took more than a year: one week to design it, fourteen months to obtain planning permission

common sight at Noel's house parties. In every sense of the phrase. But I'm not going to say anything against her. Oh, all right, then. If you insist. To be fair, Mrs Bulstrode, or Bliss, as she was dubbed by short-sighted suitors in her youth, some time last century, is nowhere near as bad as the very average female house party goer. Her taste in clothes is great. The trouble is, it's not quite great enough. Extra-whopper, mammoth, bargain-buy, Big Mac, family-pack, mega-generous would be nearer the mark.

Bliss successfully manages to forget this in her house party preparations, and the effect is akin to forcing a balloon into an old toilet roll. Such dress sense does have practical benefits, not least that house party regulars can calculate the time by checking the shade of bloodlessness in Bliss's outer limbs.

But it can be terribly embarrassing, girls; particularly if you're tempted to cram a 48DD into a 36B cup. Who can ever forget that night when Bliss had to leave Noel's Queen's Jubilee house party early, pushing the gardener's wheelbarrow before her? Well, before some of her. To her credit, she did take the wheelbarrow back the following morning. All ninety-six pieces of it. Then there was the time when –

No, I'm beginning to lose sight of the rabbit here. Who was I up to? Ah, yes – disgraced local hairdresser Diane Frizzett, the woman who wanted to become a philosopher, but failed the practical. Diane's outfit is perfectly suitable for attending house parties – if you're going as the cook. Cigarette burns and a few gravy stains can only improve it. The style is influenced by the mid-Saharan-nomad-cum-Transylvanian-émigré, with a touch of Ninja Maori thrown in for good measure – so her stylist must have been under the influence as well.

Dorothy Dosie-Pratt, the Crinkley Bottom professor's next-but-one wife and desk leg, is not an ideal sartorial example. Not any kind of example, if you ask me. Naïve? How that woman has survived to the energetically underestimated age of forty-nine is a mystery on a par with the pyramids or Crinkley Bottom's Sunday bus timetable. She doesn't so much mingle at house parties,

as negauche-iate her way about. Yes, the Great House
has got rising damp, but changing into patent leather
galoshes to dance in the ballroom is plain dotty, plain
Dotty. And that frightful red gown – one can only
imagine she chose it to match her nose. Or the Prof's
bank account after he's paid her gin bill.

Monica Zoff of the Broken Thingy Shop is a different
proposition. Not better; just different. She rolls up –
often literally – in an old boiler suit. Then there's
Crinkley Bottom's answer to Telstar, village gossip Rita
Slaghips, known as Martini because she's often drunk at
parties. This is the woman whose outfit puts the age in
cleavage: thigh-length ankle socks, tweed cowboy boots,
and a frilly vest. Do not wear the sort of clothes Rita
does to house parties! She thinks glamour's something
they teach in Japanese language classes.

Envelope collector Flo Hunniford, however, is a classic
house party role model. Noel's cook models all her rolls
on her. Ooh, no! That's unfair. Cook'd be ever so hurt.
Flo's home-made cat suit is the talk of every house
party. All the guests want to know how long it took to
make, and where she got the cats from.

One, ahem, lady you see a lot of at Noel's house
parties is Alison Wonderland. She attends only once a
year, but when she does, you see an awful lot of her.
And there's an awful lot of her to see. It's the dres, you
see. You'll note I spell it with one S; there's not enough
of it for two.

If you can imagine a lost pink handkerchief snagged
on the side of Mount Kilimanjaro, you'll understand
what I mean. It shouldn't be allowed. And Noel's in full

41

agreement with me on this. I've heard for a fact that at his last house party – the one where we auctioned the spare chambermaid – Noel was so embarrassed by Alison's dress that he spent practically the entire evening upstairs, trying to persuade her to remove it, bless him.

Another house party costume guaranteed to leave you garb-smacked belongs to councillor and producer of the *Crinkley Bottom Book of Pressed Amphibians*, Ida Knoe. How to describe Ida's bodily adornments? – Bright, colourful, flamboyant, artistic: yes, she's got some super tattoos. But her outfit is like a sleeping-sickness victim – it's not up too much.

By now, you might be gaining the slight inkling that good taste in clothes at Noel's house parties is about as rare as cat pooh at Cruft's. If so, well spotted. Good to see you're paying attention. Some of you might even be wondering just what is the right thing to wear to a house party.

I thought you'd never ask. Here's a clue. Look at the forementioned failures: Willie Touchett, Sniffer Dimbleby, Rita Slaghips, Dotty Dosie-Pratt, et al – did I mention him? Now, what do they have in common? Yes, I know. But apart from the fact that I've just mentioned them all?

I can come back in a couple of pages if you like. No? Well, I'm not surprised. This takes a heck of a lot of believing – and that's swearing! I think. The answer is that none – not one! – of them buys his or her clothes at my Wool Shop. I'll pause here while you catch your breath, have the butler bring you strong tea and smelling salts. Earth-shattering, though, isn't it? Asteroid-rattling.

Monica Zoff's boiler suit – with Lurex rivets and detachable caretaker

Star-wobbling. It could splinter Mrs Bulstrode's bodice. Almost.

Oh yes, these village worthies visit the other clothes shops in the village: Corsets in Fashion, and Threads Sales (a division of the Dud Clobber chain); even Authentic Anteeks (–Honestly!) Ltd, whose proprietor Les Dodge E. Deels puts the con into conversation piece. But, well, in Crinkley Bottom, you've either got it, or you run an establishment that isn't called the Wool Shop.

Don't misunderstand me. I'm not saying it's impossible to dress correctly for a house party if you don't buy your clothes from the Wool Shop. Goodness me, no! I'm not saying that at all. I'm writing it.

And I'm being strictly neutered when I write that the Crinkley Bottom Wool Shop has got it all: woolly waistcoats, woolly socks, woolly ballgowns, woolly brooches, woolly top hats, woolly silk gloves. Granted, the woolly fly-zips, woolly scuba suits and woolly flippers leave something to be desired, but you're not going to need them at the sort of house party Noel hosts, are you? At least, not before 1 a.m.

Even more excitingly, my assistant Anne Dye and I have set up a special department devoted solely to house party attire, and called, rather whimsically I thought, Clothed for Lunch. It's strange, but ever since she put the sign in the frosted-glass front window, we haven't had a single customer. Not that we had many before that, now I come to mention it.

Are we downhearted, though? No, we are not, for I'm sure that, having read this fair and completely unbiased piece of propaganda, you'll all come to realize that, where house parties are concerned, it's not what you buy that counts; it's where you buy it.

Now, before you all flock down to the Wool Shop, hoping to have your inside-legs measured with my woolly ruler, I must stress that I don't serve customers myself. That, like Noel, is a little beneath me. However, my assistant Anne Dye is wonderfully capable. In fact, she was only prevented from going to university by one teensy-weensy thing – her brain.

Anne can provide you with anything anyone could ever want for any house party, at any time. That is, at any time between 10 and 3, Mondays to Saturdays. Except for Thursday afternoons when she goes to have her guinea-pig dry-cleaned. And Wednesday lunchtimes when she takes her great-great-grandmother to visit the parole officer. And alternate Mondays when she helps out with Crinkley Bottom's meals-on-horseback service. And every third Saturday when she chairs the meeting of the local Every Third Saturday We Have a Meeting Society. And Tuesday mornings when she goes out and dusts the village bus queue. And every fifth Thursday morning when –

Hold on! No wonder we're not getting the customers. The blooming place is never open! I think you'd better excuse me. I need to go and have a rather stiff word with my so-called assistant. Dear me, yes. Now, where did I put that extra-long knitting needle . . . ?

INCORRECT HOUSE PARTY ATTIRE

Pru's 20 Big No-Nos

Off-the-shoulder bloomers
Baler-twine braces
Open-toed socks
Short-sleeved overcoats
Hobnailed shoulder-pads
See-through corn-plasters
Polo-neck sandals
Wooden support garments

Tie-on beauty spots
Steel–tipped bras
Single–breasted wallets
Moustache suspenders (the ladies' model)
Thermal sunglasses
Lace–up clogs
Strapless wristwatches
Tartan slacks and matching hairpieces
'I Love Noel Edmonds' T–shirts
Bell–bottomed tooth–braces
Anything not bought in the Crinkley Bottom Wool Shop

6. Preparing the Room

After punching a gnat, getting a tax refund, and buying a packet of washing powder without the word New! on it, the most difficult thing in life is overestimating the intelligence of a Crinkley Bottomer, particularly when it comes to house parties.

To demonstrate, I broke the habit of a lunchtime, went down to the Liszt and Newt, and asked the lads, 'Where do you hold it?' Ninety per cent of them said, 'In the bathroom.' Well, that's just silly. Eighty-nine per cent of them don't even have a bathroom. And anyway, where'd you put the sausage rolls? Yes, all right; same place you usually put them, only it'd be closer. But you get the point: if you're going to hold your own house party, you've got to do it in a suitable room.

At the Great House, we spent years experimenting with different settings: the cellar, the library, the ballroom, the scullery, the bedroom. None of them seemed quite right. Then one morning . . . I had a bright idea. I thought, why not try the house party room? And it worked! You'd almost think the place was made for house parties.

Unfortunately, having hit upon the appropriate room, you'll find your troubles are only just beginning. For a start, you've got to clean it. I know: the builders swore they went round with a duster after they'd built it. But the sort of folk you'll attract to your house party might just want to see the pattern on your wallpaper, or sit in a chair without having to carve a door in the dust first, or even stroll around and not get garrotted by a cobweb.

So get out the polish, kickstart the vacuum cleaner, and while you're about it, have a go at those windows. A little stained glass is OK, but you don't want people mistaking the place for Westminster Abbey.

With clean windows, you will spot a few things in the room you'd not noticed before, like daylight. There'll also be the usual family clutter carelessly flung over the furniture and floor – tights, blouses, high heels, nighties. Gather them up and give them back to your dad, then make a start on the stuff the female part of your family have left lying around.

If all this sounds onerous, it's not. It's blooming hard work. But don't get disheartened! If all the clearing and cleaning gets you down, just think of the lovely surprises you can look forward to at the end of it: food, money, fine crockery, friends you thought had gone for ever. And that's just what you're likely to find slipped down the back of your settee.

Now, at this stage, you may be wondering, sheesh! how on earth am I going to embellish the room? Well, don't. Keep your mind on what you're supposed to be reading. I've known scalded gnats with a longer attention span.

Right, with me now? You don't want to go and rearrange the cruet, or pull the spaniel a couple of millimetres closer to the television set? Oh, good. Now, once you've rid the room of any unnecessary material, it's important to bring in a few things to stimulate the intellect of the typical house party guest, like a bottle of whisky, a bottle of sherry, a bottle of port, a bottle of gin – stop gibbering. I know it's expensive, but leave an empty bucket or two in the hallway, and you might get some of it back before the night's out.

Something you may not have considered, for at least two or three paragraphs, is embellishing the room: prettifying it with beautiful objects to create an ambience, and enhance your guests' surroundings. Don't get excited; we're not back to the booze again.

There are hosts who consult their servants on this. I'm all in favour of that. In fact, I wish I could consult their servants on it. Because mine are a fat lot of use. Ask the chambermaids to summon up an ambience, and they ring the local hospital. The butler's no better. Tell him to get a florist; he orders 200 bonsai trees. So, as the indiscriminating duck plucker said, it's all down to me.

Personally, I don't go a bunch on flowers. Too limp and wimpy for someone like me, and they never match my pink slacks. My advice is to go for conversation pieces, instead. Basically, these are pieces that you can have a conversation about. Bit obvious that, really. Sorry. But they stock this book in the House of Commons library, so you've got to make allowances.

As I said, a conversation piece can be anything. No, OK, it can't be a traction engine, or an asteroid. Or Terry Nutter's dog. No, very clever. But, provided you can fit it in the room, and it doesn't smell or explode or emit life-threatening rays, a conversation piece can be anything.

Noel's conversation pieces: So successful they leave guests speechless

In theory, if you went into your garden, brained a slug with a brick, and scraped it on to your coffee table, you'd have a conversation piece. Admittedly, the conversation it produced would be short-lived and carried out in the upper ranges of the human audible register. But some hosts may prefer it that way, particularly if they get house party guests from Crinkley Bottom.

On the other hand, you may want to impress your guests; give them a taste of something rather more exclusive than a crushed slug. In other words, show off.

Noel's ancient-Roman combine harvester: A conversation piece which has prompted such discursive gems as 'Aargh! My nose!' and 'Quick! Phone a doctor'

This isn't the motivation behind my selection of conversation pieces, naturally. No, it's not. I just, er, well yes, OK, it is. But I don't go over the top into gauchery. Someone who makes sure of that is Crinkley Bottom's doyen of good taste, proprietor of Authentic Anteeks (– Honestly!) Ltd, Les Dodge E. Deels.

Where conversation pieces are concerned, Noel believes taste is very important. All his taste of peppermint

What can I say about Les? – Big, gruff, bearded, beer belly, bald spot. She's a funny woman. But she has this nose for digging out archaeological treasures – it saves her buying a spade. And some of the conversation pieces she's put my way have been nothing short of incredible. Literally. If I say it was Les who sold me Queen Victoria's first driving licence, and the bottle of shampoo Yul Brynner used during the filming of *The King and I*, you'll see what I mean.

Les also came up trumps for my Queen's Jubilee

house party with Mother Theresa's hip flask, a signed photograph of Robin Hood, two prehistoric cornflake bowls, and a piece of King Arthur's round table – with the original tomato ketchup stains still on it!

Over the years, Les has kept the conversation pieces coming, still more astonishing in their fascination and exclusivity: Sherlock Holmes's pipe, George Eliot's razor, a sixteenth-century car alarm, Count Dracula's crucifix, and a Rottweiler fossil.

Only last month she came up with the skull of Genghis Khan, dating from his death in 1227 – and a smaller one of his from when he was a boy; also a dinosaur feather, René Descartes's suspender belt, a medieval police helmet, a West Ham season ticket belonging to Wolfgang Amadeus Mozart, a piece of the ozone hole, a Swiss Navy flag, and Joan of Arc's rugby boots – which came as a real surprise; I never knew she'd even been to Rugby.

Next week, Les flies to Rome to acquire my conversation *pièce de résistance*, Pope Pius XII's cigarette lighter. In her own jet. The woman is quite unbelievable. Her shop in Crinkley Bottom has built up a large and highly select clientèle. Trades Descriptions officers are regular visitors, and the local CID just can't seem to keep away.

It's unlikely you'll be fortunate enough to have a branch of Les's Authentic Anteeks (– Honestly!) Ltd in your village, but don't give up hope. In view of the money she's had off me lately, it's only a matter of time before you do.

Inevitably, with envied conversation pieces such as

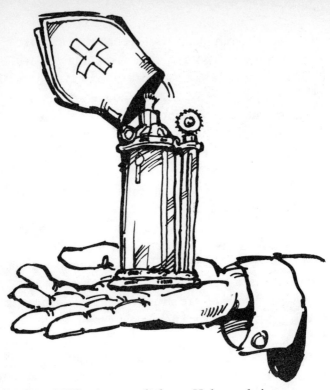

Pope Pius XII's cigarette lighter: Holy smoke!

mine in the room, the question arises: should you think about insurance? The answer's no, not unless you're having trouble sleeping. As for actually taking out insurance, this is a good idea. Don't, however, pay any heed to these people who tell you honesty's the best policy. At a house party, the best policy's one that covers you against fire, theft and rock stars.

Having paid for the insurance, then, and been discharged from the acute shock unit of your local

The complex underlying symbolism of Noel's conversation pieces can be surprising. This is actually three balloons tied to an iron

hospital, you should now turn your attention to selecting the finishing touches for your room.

I always choose a couple of dozen cushions for mine, but that's only because the Crinkley Bottom Army Surplus Store has run out of sandbags. Yes, I'm ashamed to say that as house parties progress up at the Great House, certain guests exhibit a tendency to indulge in snide comments, personal abuse and gratuitous physical violence. I wouldn't mind, but it's always directed at me.

Joan of Arc's rugby boots: The only studs you're likely to find at the Great House

Anyone'd think they'd never been charged for their drinks before.

What you select for your own room's finishing touches – first aid kit, stretcher, stand-by emergency surgical team – is up to you. It's sensible, though, always to distribute a number of heavy literary works about the room. You know the sort of thing: Tolstoy's *War and Peace*, Velikovsky's *Worlds in Collision*, the *Crinkley Bottom Observer*'s Sunday supplement. Not only does this provide your high-brow guests with something to browse through, it gives everyone the idea that someone in your house can actually read. Culture cred's important at house parties.

Rather less challenging literary material (it's no good

asking me for examples here, I'm afraid) may be made available for your more common guests. Leave it under the tables where they're most likely to find it.

And that's it. As the contagious diseases doctor said to the bishop, there you have it: one house party room, clean, clear, bright, well stocked and appointed; just poised for the magic moment when your house party guests arrive and begin mingling, getting to know one another, having a few drinks, getting to know one another better, having a few more drinks, getting to know one another even better, having few door mrinks, growing five pairs of extra hands, having a drew four minks, disappearing down behind the furniture, having a mew door frinks, checking to see one another's buttons are still functioning, having . . . Er, look, maybe it wasn't such a good idea to clean those windows, after all.

RARE CONVERSATION PIECES

Noel's Sure-Fire Top 20

A grammatical greengrocer's sign
A football manager's long-service medal
A toothbrush not recommended by dentists
A Skoda driver's speeding ticket
A sunburnt bat
A one-way ticket to Milton Keynes
A Scottish beermat with an orange-juice stain on it
An unpersonalized Bentley number plate
A hedgehog with a sense of humour
A bottle of Crinkley Bottom aftershave
A well-trodden police boot
An orally resuscitated swordfish
An American movie star's golden wedding anniversary
    card
A receipt for sunburn lotion from a Skegness shop
A Hell's Angel's dry-cleaning ticket
A local-radio DJ's MENSA certificate
A Crinkley Bottom Wonderers' cupwinner's medal
A kamikaze pilot's pension book
An uncracked Ford Capri wing mirror
A Crinkley Bottomer's dog that doesn't know its way
    to the Liszt and Newt

7. What to Eat

The Great House's Queen of Cuisine, cook
Flossiebel d'Uff-Baker, dons her floral PVC apron
and matching oven gloves to handle some hot
potatoes on house party food

**What food do you usually prepare for house
parties?**
Oh, lots, m'dear. Let me see, now, there's cheese flan,
cheese pie, cheese soufflé, cheese pâté, cheese trifle,
cheese soup, cheese haggis, cheese-on-toast, cheese and
biscuits, cheese and sausage. Oh, and cheese and cheese,
in a cheese base, with a delicious light savoury garnish –
of cheese.

**You find cheese a convenient food for house parties,
then?**
Don't know about that, m'dear, but it's very handy. At
the Great House, we get it delivered by the old Crinkley
Bottom milkman, look-you.

You get your cheese delivered by the milkman?
We do, m'dear. In bottles. 'Course, it wasn't cheese
when he started out with it.

Is house party food expensive?
Only if you buy it, m'dear. What I mean is, there's lots
of lovely foods free in the countryside, if you just take
the trouble to look for them.

E.g.?
Yes, that's one. But shouldn't you spell it EGG? No
matter. We're very lucky here with so much natural food
all around us. There's the Crinkley Bottom hedgehog,
look-you. That's the one that hibernates in summer.

**How on earth do your house party guests eat
hedgehog?**
Very carefully, m'dear. But for guests who prefer a little
more meat on the bone, I send our apprentice poacher Trev
out for a Crinkley Bottom bull. It's a kindness, really; poor
things keep getting chased by people crossing their field.

Are they good value?
Gracious, yes, look-you! I made 600 beefburgers out of
the last one.

That sounds like an awful lot of bull.
No, m'dear, it's perfectly true.

**Could you recommend any, em, slightly more
conventional local delicacies?**
Crinkley Bottom moles are a particular favourite of mine.
Trev has great fun climbing the trees to catch them. No?
Well, how about the Crinkley Bottom hopping snake.
No? Er, the great spotted zebra? The desert tadpole?
The monochrome peacock? The myopic eagle? – lovely
with a little brandy butter and cheese. Coo, you're a
pernickity old so-and-so and no mistake.

**Is there no normal edible wildlife in Crinkley
Bottom?**
There's snails, m'dear. Leastways, there would be if we
were fast enough to catch them.

Surely you could catch something from the River Crinkle?
Oh, you can catch plenty from the River Crinkle: dysentery, cholera, typhoid, mange . . .

Do you buy any food at all for your house parties?
Oh, dearie me, yes, look-you. Noel's food bill for a single house party comes to around £50. 'Course, he doesn't spend as much on his guests' food.

Is foreign produce suitable for a house party?
Personally, I never buy anything from New Zealand, m'dear – in case it's bad and I've got to go back and change it. So we get most of our food from the Crinkley Bottom grocer's. On Tick.

You have an account there, then?
No, Tick's the grocer's horse. Arnie rides her up with our order. Arnie's Crinkley Bottom's well-qualified delivery boy – got an A level in Whistling, look-you.

Do the house party guests give you any food?
Only raspberries.

Do you have a microwave?
Oh no, m'dear. I just like it short on top and curly at the sides.

I mean, how do you prepare your house party food? Do you braise, broil, baste?
No. Generally, I just cook it.

How much time do you put into food preparation?
None at all. I don't hold with herbs, m'dear.

*Flossiebel d'Uff-Baker: Meals like Mother used to make –
before she was arrested for poisoning*

**To put it another way, how long do you allow
yourself to prepare a house party repast?**
Hours, m'dear, because there's such a lot to do, see –
rolling, beating, tossing, kneading, stuffing. And that's
just putting my apron on.

What does Noel like to eat?
Food, generally.

Can you be more precise?
Yes. Food, specifically.

I believe Noel has very high food standards?
That's about the only thing he's got that's high, m'dear.
But yes, Noel is a noted scoffer. Hereabouts, he's known
as the man who puts the gnome into gastronome. He
can't cook for toffee, though – thinks rice pudding was a
mad Russian monk.

**How much thought do you put into what you serve
at house parties?**
Absolute minutes, m'dear! You can't just throw
ingredients together willy-nilly, look-you. They have to
be subtly interlinked by a single culinary theme. I usually
choose things beginning with B. You know: Brussels,
broccoli, bacon, bloaters, brown rice, beetroot, bakewell
tart, Big Mac, bits of cheese.

**This B theme runs through all your Great House
meals, does it?**
Normally, m'dear. Except for breakfasts. They always
begin with T.

T?
Or coffee.

Is hygiene important?
Crucial. I wash all Noel's guests before I let them get
anywhere near my food.

Have you had any experience of vegans?
No, m'dear. I've only got a bicycle.

**Vegans – people who don't eat meat or dairy
products.**
Oh no, Noel doesn't invite the poor. I think he's worried
it might be catching.

What about utensils?
I had them out with my adenoids when I was twelve,
m'dear.

**You misunderstand me. I'm inquiring whether it's
important to have the proper equipment.**
Oooo, I say! Lawks a'mercy! Well, I never! What a qu –!

**Let, let me put it another way. Should house party
food be prepared with special knives and forks and
so on?**
Not necessarily, m'dear. If I couldn't find my carving
knife at a house party, look-you, I'd use Pru's tongue.
No, no, only joking; I wouldn't do that. It'd turn the
meat.

**Do kitchen gadgets have a place in your house
party preparations?**
Good Lord, yes. Usually at the back of the cupboard
under the sink.

Would you care to elucidate?
Very kind, m'dear, but I went before we started.

That's to say, what gadgets do you employ?
Oh, I don't employ them, look-you. Look a bit silly
giving my can-opener a wage packet at the end of the
week, wouldn't I? Not that the blooming thing'd be able
to open it, if I did. I'm not bitter, though, m'dear. Noel
provides me with some extremely useful kitchen gadgets
– at very reasonable rates.

Go on.
No, it's true!

I mean, go on about your gadgets.
Oh, I see. Well, there's my Julian Clary. I call it that
because it's a mincer. I give them all names, look-you.
Like Tuck – that's my frier. And King Kong, the griller.

Do you employ, er, use a sweet trolley?
Well, I think it's sweet, m'dear. It's got this ormolu
handle, see, with nice pink little wheels, and Tiddler's
Lake skating scenes on the sides. And it's self-lowering,
look-you.

And can you higher it?
Ooh, yes. Noel charges £10 a week, or 20p per bun.

**There's been a lot of talk lately about the Crinkley
Sandwich – mainly in the local courts. Where does
Noel stand on it?**
In the bathroom, m'dear, to see in his shaving mirror.

**Your name and the Crinkley Sandwich are often
mentioned in the same mouthful – can you tell us
something of its mysterious history?**
It goes back to the Fourth Earl of Crinkley, around
1750. That's ten to eight in today's money.

He was a gambler, wasn't he?
Well, he'd have to be to eat something like that, m'dear.
Legend has it, he was so fond of gambling, he wanted
something he could eat without having to leave his card
game.

So he invented the Crinkley Sandwich?
No, he invented the edible table. In time, though, it was
refined into what became known as the Crinkley

The Crinkley Sandwich: From a photofit currently in the hands of Scotland Yard's Lethal Weapons Unit

Sandwich – originally, a piece of bread between two slices of ham. 'Course, it's changed lots since then.

Can you tell us its present ingredients – either the leaded or the unleaded version?
Coo, I don't rightly know that I should repeat them, m'dear. It's not as if it's after 9 p.m., look-you.

But you have seen fit to serve the Crinkley Sandwich at house parties?
Ah now, that was before the EC ruling that it was only suitable for use on the trains.

As travellers' snacks?
As railway sleepers, m'dear.

Is the Crinkley Sandwich safe to serve at house parties?
Oh yes–on–the–Richter–scale, m'dear. There is absolutely nothing whatsoever wrong with serving the Crinkley Sandwich at a house party. I'd draw the line at actually eating it, though.

Does Crinkley Sandwich consumption occur at Noel's house parties?
You're not from the police, are you, m'dear? Are you sure? Only you're asking an awful lot of questions. Ah, good. Well, yes, several of Shorty's – I mean Noel's – guests have dabbled with the Crinkley Sandwich. Nothing serious, mind. There's no shoving goes on, and Noel insists they, well, do it outside, away from the canary and Pru. The Great House is strictly a Crinkley-Sandwich-free zone.

Is it true that the Government has banned the Crinkley Sandwich from certain areas?
That's right – the mouth, the throat, and the stomach. Came as a devastating blow to many people, m'dear; the Crinkley Bottom Indigestion Tablet Company, for one.

Finally, Mrs d'Uff-Baker, for anyone planning their own house party food, have you any tips to offer them?
Oh, yes, m'dear.

. . . Well, what are they?

They're asparagus, m'dear. Nice and green and firm and – Hang on, m'dear. What are you doing with my carving knife? You could do someone a nasty –

(Readers interested in applying for the unexpectedly vacant post of Noel's cook are invited to write to The Great House, Crinkley Bottom, Crinkleyshire, BC1 1NE.)

8. Crinkley Pottage

One of the great recipes as prepared by Cook

YE OLDE GREYTE HOWSE POTTAGE
(authentic Crinkley Bottom recipe, circa 1647)

Ye ingreedi-ents
15lb Mutton from a Pygge.
A halfe a sacke of ye fineste goats.
2lb filleted coddefyshe. Remove bones.
A Guinea Fowle – or cheaper if avaylable.
An large Turnippe, well mash-ed, then diced into
    quarters.
An Ox's dangly-bittes.
2 large lintels.
6 Bigge Mackes.
A large Woodcock, or a real one, if to hand.
16 bulbs of ye fineste Garlicke and a large packette of
    Clorettes.
Ye liver of an Haggis.
A broth of an Irishmanne.
Half a pinte of dripping from an incontinente rabbitte.
A dozen Sheep's Egges, coddled.
6 curlers and a sniper. (That is, 6 *curlews* and a *Snipe.*)
A large thrutch of possetted twassets.
An Packette of Knorre Instante Mushroome Soupe. (Not
    ye contentes, just ye packette, twerppe!)
Ye breast of a Big Bustard – ye bigger ye Bustard ye
    better.

An indefinite artickle with ye seeds removed.
12 bottels of Syruppe of Figges.
Ye gizzard of a Doris.
An bucket of Garni.
An Large Sicke-bagge.

Ye methodde
Assemble ingreedients in a large vassall by light of
waning moon or waxing ear. Stirre well until ye blinke.
Boille ye pottage vigorously over a low light – or Gas
Marke 5 on ye olde microwave. Skim ye scum. Test
frequently with elbow. Plucke a live goose to add to ye
potte. Phone ambulance to take ye to hospitalle to sew
fingers backe on. Send for takeawaye. (Serves 27.)

9. Breaking the Ice

Everything is ready, the guests are arriving in droves – some of them in cars – now all you have to do is break the ice.

In the grand old heydays of house parties, Great-Uncle Ebeneezer Edmonds would home in on a newly arrived guest, slap him or her heartily on the back or front, and bellow, 'Excuse the cold hands – I've just been identifying Granddad.'

The guest, startled rather by Ebeneezer's energetic salutation and un-Edmonds-like honesty, would invariably choke on his or her post-prandial tipple, crunching the icecubes and jettisoning them, along with any loose teeth, over Eb in a shotgun-blast of sparkling cold shards. Guests from the immediate area would rally around with their best handkerchiefs and frowns, mopping and worrying, and before you could say infidelity, everyone was talking and laughing and getting on like a chip pan on fire.

Thus, the expression breaking the ice entered the language. It was a clever ruse of Great-Uncle Ebeneezer's, and rarely kept him hospitalized for more than a week.

Etiquette at house parties these days is different, alas,

although the need to break the ice, metaphorically speaking, remains. Before we go any further, though, I think it's only fair to warn you of something.

Breaking the ice at modern house parties is not a lot of things. It's not inky, it's not deciduous, it's not mauve, it's not tadpoly, it's not a small fat pixie sitting on a toadstool. But the main thing it's not, is easy. Breaking the ice at house parties today is harder than a Crinkley Café meat pie. And the reason is, it actually involves you, as host, approaching a guest, or a group of them (technically known as a whinney, blather or bulstrode), and, well, talking.

You remember talking. 'Course you do. It's in the dictionary between shouting and whispering. Used to be popular as a form of conversation before the multi-purpose grunt was invented. Little old ladies still do it. To their cats.

No? Oh, come on! You must have seen people doing it on television. One chap opens his mouth and sort of jiggles his vocal cords to make word noises. Another does the same thing, only louder. A fight breaks out; they have a car chase; his girlfriend breaks her high-heel on the way to the helicopter; and the coffee adverts come on. Well, the first bit: that's it – talking.

It's not quite as straightforward as you see on the telly. Nowadays, there's an art to talking. It involves beginning every response with 'Well, I mean', finishing it with 'Innit?' and machine-gunning the space in between with 'Sort of', 'Kind of', 'Sort-of-like-kind-of', 'Thingy', 'Whatsit', 'Errr', and 'You know'.

Saying anything half-way meaningful in addition to

these verbal zimmer-frames is optional and considered something of an unexpected bonus. Prime examples of this glorious style in action can be had by listening to the DJs of Crinkley Bottom's pop radio station, CB FM, on 2 MHz VHF, or Deaf Wish II, as it's known.

It doesn't end there, oh no. Posh people have to say 'Absolutely', 'Basically', 'Actually' and 'Awfully' an awful lot. And politicians are not permitted to utter more than seven words without using a 'Clearly', an 'Obviously', an 'Of course', an 'At the end of the day', or a lie. And if possible all five together at once.

Petty officials must by law stress only the prepositions in their sentences, and say 'i.e.', 'e.g.', and 'et cetera', even though most don't know how to spell them.

Ordinary people such as you and I – well, you – must say 'Myself' when they mean 'Me', and 'Me' when they mean 'I'. It also helps to use phrases with unnecessary words in them, for example 'Meet up with', 'Follow along behind', 'At this moment in time', 'A young girl of six', and 'The taller of the two egg plants'. But this is not strictly necessary, essential, compulsory, crucial, required, vital, *de rigueur*, mandatory, called for, or unforgoable. So much for me daring to open my mouth ever again.

They're the rules of talking, then. So – how do you do it? When do you do it? And who – whoops! whom – do you do it with?

Well, you don't do it like that, for a start. Most house party guests have slightly fewer than two mouths, and an annoying inability to answer more than one question at once. In Crinkley Bottom, they're not even that good. So keep it, like the inhabitants of that village, simple.

We'll start with how to do it. Talking to people is tricky. No, I'm not being faceesh, fashiet, I'm not joking. I well remember my first house party – it must have been in the sixties. Or maybe it was warmer than that. There was this very pretty girl, all by herself in the corner. Every time I passed by, carrying a surrender note from the dining-table or the *Crinkley Bottom Observer*'s editor by the feet, her eyes would follow me until I was out of sight. Oh! how I wish I'd had the courage to turn around, go over and tell her to mind her own business.

Courage, you see: that's what's needed to walk up and talk to strange people. And you'll get plenty of strange people at house parties, if mine are anything to go by.

Courage is like an eight-foot tall chicken; you have to pluck it up. You can practise this in your bedroom by strolling up to the full-length mirror, wobbling your head, and engaging your reflection in jaunty banter as though it were a house party guest. This builds confidence, and gives you valuable time to plan the menu in the padded cell you're sent to when one of the family walks in and catches you at it.

The next problem is what to say. It's not a bit of use walking up to a guest and standing there mouthing gobfuls of nothingness. They'll think you've a gherkin caught under your top plate. Make sure, therefore, there's always a scintillating opening line dancing on the tip of your tongue prior to your approach.

The nature of this remark needs some thought. It doesn't exactly get the conversation off to a flying start to come out with such gems as 'The upstairs lav's blocked with Cook's iced buns again', 'Can you see anything on my shoe?' or 'Watch your head; Flossie Rantzen's still not had that boil lanced'.

One method many hosts adopt is to lob across the conversational net a topic about which guests are likely to have strong negative feelings, such as Crinkley Bottom Wonderers' recent decision to charge for season tickets.

It's remarkable how ready people are to sound off about something they hate. You should see the number of irate telephone calls we get about that smarmy little berk after Noel's House Party's been on TV. It's amazing; I never realized Mister Blobby was so unpopular. Hoped and prayed he was, maybe.

Predicting what people will revile can be a chancy enterprise. Between you and me and the train passenger who's reading this over your shoulder, I've heard that there are some misguided souls who even find my pullovers less than fulsome. I've jotted down a few hates, however, which from experience appear to be held in general low esteem throughout the civilized world, and many parts of Crinkley Bottom. In strict tooth-gnashing order, they are:

1 Electric hand-driers that cut out eight seconds before your hands are dry.
2 50p-off coupons you have to cut up half your newspaper to get at.
3 Milk cartons you need two Land Rovers and a controlled nuclear explosion to open.
4 New biros which refuse to produce a worm's willie of ink, then leak all over your pocket when you take them back to the shop.

5   Apertures in dogs.
6   The ability of postmen to whistle at seven o'clock in the morning.
7   Alarm clocks that can't remember it's the weekend.
8   The next-door neighbour's hi-fi system.
9   Sauce bottles you can't pick up without coating the upper half of your body with sticky brown smodge.
10 Toilet paper you can spit through.

Shrewd house party hosts like to have several strings to their bows – although quite a few prefer not to wear a bow at all. If you're one of the former, you'll no doubt be interested in a method of breaking the ice which has served the Edmonds family well for forty years. Don't get too excited; we've actually been using it for more than three centuries.

Its instigator was my innumerably great-grandmother, Dame Lucrezia Edmonds, a peevish and bitter woman who kept baby crocodiles in the guests' lavatory bowl. She now haunts the Great House Longish Gallery, carrying her husband's head under her arm.

But back to Dame Lucrezia's ice-breaking ploy. In a word, insults. What better, mused Lucrezia, for producing mouth-to-mouth presuscitation than a little insult? I know! she thought, a great big insult.

You must remember that Multi-Great-Gran Lu lived in a time when the fastest form of personal transport was the banana skin. Consequently, she had to break the house party ice among guests picked from the local somewhat dozy and sleepy Crinkley Bottom villagers; or Coma-sapiens, as they're known.

Lucrezia's initial forays into shaking her guests out of their stupor – 'Don't tell me – you're from Rent-a-Peasant?', 'Who did your hair – a robin?' and 'It was a joke when I said come in fancy dress, you know' – were a little too rude-imentary, and swiftly supplanted by the meatier, spicier 'The last time I saw a jersey that size, it had udders', 'Have your legs always been that shape, or did you come on a horse?' and 'You can take your veil off, madam; we've got our mirrors insured.'

Over time, if Crinkley Bottom employers will pardon the expression, the ice-breaking insults were honed to a cutting collection of barbed beauties, to wit:

'Have you considered the police force? At least they give you clothes that match.'

'I see we've caught you in the middle of decorating.'

'Not keeping you from anything, are we – like a visit to the launderette?'

'That's a rather flamboyant tie, sir. In Crinkley Bottom, we call them towels.'

'That's a marvellously loose outfit. What happened to the fez?'

'What do you use for a fabric softener – razor blades?'

'The diet didn't work, then?'

'You look like a well-dressed man; or, to be precise, you look like a man who dressed in a well.'

'Lovely jewellery. Let's hope these hot lights don't melt it.'

'I think you're the first person we've had who can cut his toenails without taking his shoes off.'

Latter-day Lucrezias in clan Edmonds tend to plump, or more aptly plumb, for slicker, more biting barbs, along the lines of 'So sackcloth's back in, is it?', 'Is that acne, or did you sneeze in your soup?' and 'I don't suppose you need a satellite dish with ears like that.'

If these fail to spark a response, rumours abound that certain Edmondses actually resort to 'Do you find this look encourages people to give you money?', or 'Shouldn't you be getting on with something – like evolution?', or 'Would you like a handkerchief – or shall I just call Dynorod?', or even 'That's a best mohair pullover, isn't it? Have you tried to sue the goat?' Although, if true, none of them has yet lived to tell the tale.

Dodgy business, then, this talking. And as such, it's vital to select the correct guest to do it with. In Crinkley Bottom, the choice is almost made for you: 30 per cent of the guests are intoxicated; 30 per cent are incoherent; and the other two-thirds are innumerate. Add to this the fact that the local life-assurance salesman sneaks around trying to avoid talking to people, while the accountant is out leading a conga around the Pea Shoppe roof, and you'll understand why I've little option but to break the ice with my old friend Clodaugh Bumpin-Melons.

You yourself will likely be faced with a choice of potential ice breakees somewhat broader than Miss Bumpin-Melons. Well, maybe not broader, but there'll certainly be more of them. It's up to you to prune these to a harmless handful, a task which may be expedited by immediately discounting the kind of guest who kicks open the door and exclaims, 'Where do we throw the car keys, then?', or 'I say! look what I ran over on the way here.'

Out of the frame, too, should be anyone who has hooded eyelids, tattooed teeth, insecticide-scented hair, twin puncture marks on their throat, a habit of constantly scratching anything below the waistline – whether it belongs to them or not, straps on the arms of their jackets, machine-gun-shaped objects in their pockets, plasma-stained toecaps, Sicilian bodyguards, or bagpipes.

A form of guest you, regrettably, must face up to at some stage is the chap whom the tactful house party host describes as over-emotional. I'm going to call him drunk as a skunk. He's taken the wrong turning on his way to your bathroom, climbed all 937 – or is it 938? – steps of the spiral staircase in your padlocked west wing, and just happened upon your best whisky supply.

There is no way you can avoid this sort of guest, although it is occasionally possible to take evasive action when he swings by on the chandelier. Getting into conversation with him is no problem. Getting out of it's nothing to worry about, either, as it's only a matter of time before he folds himself into seventeen pieces and becomes part of the floor. It's the bit in between you might have trouble with.

Guests such as this use a universal language known as Drunkasaskunkese; *Drunchashershkuncheesh*, in the native tongue. It engages shortly after their thirteenth unit of alcohol, or about five minutes into the average house party.

If you are to understand this guest and communicate to him the concept that if he comes within binocular distance of your house again you'll personally bite his head off at the ankles, it's essential to acquaint yourself with the fundaments of his vocabulary, namely:

Barsh nash: A novel method of acquiring calories in a pub which actually involves chewing.

Crishpsh: The generic term given to a lipshmacking form of barsh nash, varieties of which include Cheesher Nunion, Before Tomato, and Zoltan Finger. For most Drunkasaskunk speakers, it takes considerably longer to ask for a packish of crishpsh than to eat one.

Peas: A perishable commodity which, combined with quiet, is essential for survival the morning after the night before.

Quiche: Tiny, mountain-range-shaped metal objects that turn your car on, and invariably disappear after about ten pints. Not to be confused with 'quiches': savoury cheese and bacon snacks which invariably reappear after about ten pints.

Drinking-up time: The time allowed to knock back a pint at the conclusion of licensing hours. Legally, ten minutes; theoretically, two point four seconds; practically, an hour; probably, longer.

Alcoholic: A Drunkasaskunk speaker you don't like who drinks as much as you do.

Head: The thick insubstantial thing you drink your pint through.

Tipshy: What you feel after five pints.

Dishy: What you feel after six pints.

Double: What you see after seven pints.

Starsh: What you see after eight pints.

Pleesh ociffer: What sees you after nine pints.

Short: What you are after you've paid the fine.

The drinksh are on me: A phrase uttered when alcohol intake is beginning to have a serious effect on both the wallet and the brain.

Mine's a large one: A vulgar boast, or a request for alcohol when it's not your round. No matter what difficulty the Drunkasaskunk speaker is having pronouncing other words, these four always seem to be enunciated perfectly.

Mush: A reference to a great quantity – generally of ladies or money, best exemplified in the traditional bar-room questions: 'Getting mush?' or 'How mush do I owe you?' – neither of which is ever answered with mush degree of accurashy. Also a vivid description of most Barsh Nash.

A lav . . . : The beginning of a request made prior to choosing a drink.

Gish . . . : The beginning of a request made prior to being thrown out.

Hangover: A condition which affects the Drunkasaskunk speaker's head, and describes his stomach.

Abstinence: A beneficial thing, provided it's practised in moderation.

One for the road: A common expression, used on innumerable occasions in the course of an evening – often by the same person – and heralding a serious attempt to leave the premises before dawn.

Drunk: The unfortunate condition of your friends and your pint.

Sloshed: A sensation of semi-conscious dismay and disorientation, derived from the foreign word 'Schlossed',

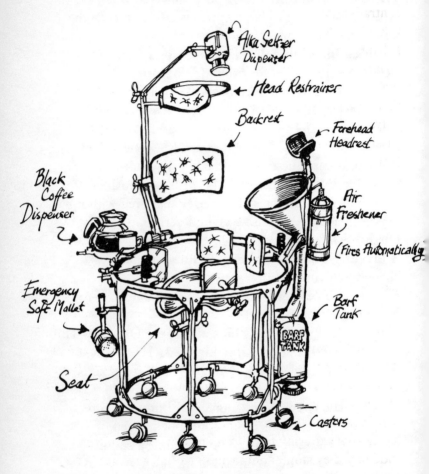

Alka Seltzer Dispenser

Head Restrainers

Backrest

Forehead Headrest

Black Coffee Dispenser

Air Freshener

(Fires Automatically)

Emergency Soft Mallet

Barf Tank

Seat

Casters

Newt-mobile: Transporting guests home by Uncle Ebeneezer's Newt-mobile usually took about a week – ten minutes for the journey, six days working out how to get them out of it meaning to be hit on the head by a German castle.

I've had enough, thanksh: A desperate plea to be contradicted.

What do you mean, how come I'm such an expert on Drunkasaskunkese? Yes, I have been known to breach the portals of Crinkley Bottom's Liszt and Newt public house on occasion. Someone has to go in and rescue the Salvation Army girls. I've seen some pretty bad cases of passive drinking in there, believe you me. Satisfied? Yes, you are. Right, let's get on. You've wasted more than enough of this page already; and I've yet to address the cosmically important aspects of breaking the ice at house parties, like, er . . . well, there's the, um . . . No, I think that's just about it: plucking up courage, picking your target, practising wobbling your head, planning your opening line.

Now, all you have to do is pray that your ice breakee isn't one of those appalling people who just go on and on, never knowing when to stop, and refusing to come to the end of a sentence – without tacking a bit on the end, so that you begin to suspect they're breathing through their ears, because there's simply no way any normally aspirated human being could keep up such a torrential flow of words without turning blue at the edges and keeling over backwards suffering from oxygen starvation, and then suddenly they stop! – only you're so shocked that before you've had time to say anything, they're off again, rambling on and on and on about something else and hello what's this . . . ?

BORING GUESTS?
Noel's Top 20 Conversation Stoppers

Where do people from Coventry send people they're not speaking to?

Why do all Chinese names sound like ricochets?

How come you can never get the last bit of soap to stick to the new bar?

Where did people put their windows before walls were invented?

What's the point of a map of Venus?

If spiders were really meant to catch flies, why don't they have wings?

Haven't words been around long enough to spell themselves by now?

If God owns all the world and everything in it, what do you buy Him for Christmas?

How come you never hear birds breaking wind?

Do policemen keep thinking members of the public are looking older?

How can one box of matches have an average number of contents?

Why don't scientists stop trying to produce more houses and fuel and food, and just find a way to shrink everyone?

How come your ears are always the right distance apart to fit your head between?

Why do people say a coat's hanging up when any fool can see it's hanging down?

Who's this fellow called Will, and why does everyone keep shooting at him?

What did the man to buy the first radio tune in to?

How long was it before primitive men realized that the
   first people to die weren't just heavy sleepers?
Why doesn't slippery mean like a slipper?
Why does food only fall off your fork *after* you've moved
   it away from the plate?
How come small spiders never get stuck in the bath?

10. Etiquette

'Only pheasants attend dinner in braces . . .' as my Great-Uncle Ebeneezer used to say. There is always a concern that once the guests have arrived and the ice has been ceremoniously broken, sudden and unexpected breaches of etiquette can take place. Here are some of the tell-tale signs to watch out for.

If there's one thing that I personally pride myself on, it's my table manners. In fact, when it comes to formal dining, I am a veritable stickler for etiquette. 'Manners Maketh Man, er, and Woman, of course' is an old dictum, but nonetheless one that is strictly adhered to in the Edmonds household.

When you're an example-setter like me, people expect you to be a fount of knowledge on etiquette, style and taste. Well, let's face it – since Noel Coward popped his clogs, there's only me left really, isn't there? There must be something inbred in us Noels, some genetic piece of the Great Cosmic Jigsaw Puzzle that makes us leaders in the field. Did I mention that Babs (Cartland) regularly consults me on which fish fork to use? But enough tales out of school.

You see, from the humblest WI tea party to the Lord Mayor's Banquet, I've been there with the highest in the land and never disgraced myself once, I'm proud to say.

Well, admittedly, there *was* that *one* occasion when I inadvertently tucked the tablecloth into my trouser-top and walked away at the end of the meal, dragging the contents of the table on to the floor with a resounding crash.

Luckily, there was no one there of any importance – indeed, Her Majesty herself never batted an eyelid. I know what you're thinking – that sort of thing could happen to any house party guest. As, I suppose, could the time when, at another function, the pickled onion I was chasing round my plate flicked into the air and landed in the cleavage of a well-known politician's wife. Needless to say, I knew the correct table etiquette and warmed my hands on the candelabra before retrieving it.

Luckily, her husband saw the funny side and just blacked the one eye instead of both of them.

As one old retired Colonel said at the time as he slapped me on the back: 'I don't recognize the face, old boy, but the table manners are familiar.' Then he muttered something about keeping pigs, which I didn't quite catch at the time. Yes, I place great store on politeness and insist on correct behaviour at my house parties here in Crinkley Bottom.

I've been brought up that way. My mother, God bless her, taught me to eat properly with a knife and fork as soon as we could afford them. The lads in the Secondary Modern sixth form were really impressed when I proudly displayed my new-found ability.

Since then, I've made a study of the subject and there's nothing I don't know about it, even down to which sleeve you should wipe your mouth on after eating greasy food with your hands.

Indeed, my table manners have even been commented upon by the local Crinkley Bottom gentry. Only the other day, Lady Veronica Haddem, who had invited me to her home – Haddem-Hall-in-the-Woods – for the occasion of the annual Hunt Supper, took me to one side at the end of the evening and muttered: 'Mr Edmonds, you have the manners of a boor.'

Naturally, I thanked her profusely for comparing me so favourably with the South Africans who, as we all know, are a veritable model of politeness and civility. As an extra-civil touch, I expressed my gratitude for a marvellous evening and, as I recall, her exact words to me were: 'You might like to wait until you get an invitation next time.'

So impressed were the other members of the Hunt that they have invited me as a special guest to their next gathering of horse and hounds, and the Master himself even promised to give me 'a good ten minutes' start', whatever that means. So that's something to look forward to.

As good hosts always set an example, I am willing to share my expert knowledge and pass on the following tips you might care to circulate among your guests to enable your dinner party to take place in a civilized manner.

First things first.

Let them know that, it being a formal occasion, the right dress will be required. Impress on them that in the words on your gilt-edged invitation card which state: DRESS, DJ refers to the fact that dinner jackets are required to be worn,

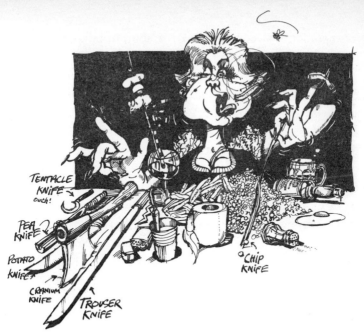

TENTACLE KNIFE
ouch!

PEA KNIFE

POTATO KNIFE

CRANIUM KNIFE

TROUSER KNIFE

CHIP KNIFE

Noel's First Law of Food Preservation: The more confusing the choice of cutlery, the less time a guest has to eat your food

not donkey jackets, as I once mistakenly thought when I did not have as much *savoir-faire* as what I have now.

(Luckily, the function I attended wearing the donkey jacket was a Crinkley Bottom TV dinner, so the other guests were all too drunk to notice.)

Now to the meal itself. Supposing the repast starts with soup. Let your guests know that testing the temperature of the soup with the tip of the elbow is frowned upon – as is fanning the soup with a toupée or a pair of underpants in order to cool it down.

If someone is consuming their soup in an unseemly and vociferous manner, ask them to at least try to keep in tempo with the string quartet. I find the Radetzky March is a good one for slurping the Brown Windsor to.

Eating irons – I mean cutlery – can pose major problems. If a guest seems unsure of which knife and fork to use, hint that they should watch which ones their neighbour uses. Stress that by this you do not mean Mrs Fairclough from Number 62, but the person sitting next to them.

I don't know about you, but most people find knives a major problem. There are all sorts of knives that can make an appearance on the dining-table: butter knives, fish knives, steak knives, paring knives, carving knives, jelly knives, soup knives, even flick-knives at some of the dos I've been to at Terry Nutter's. The list is endless.

Some are easily identifiable – others not so. Here are a few you should make your visitors familiar with.

The knife which is four feet long with a little point on the end is in fact the trouser knife. This is to enable you to slip the knife down your trousers and scratch your ankle while holding a conversation at the same time.

The knife which is the same size as an ordinary table-knife but which has a hollow indentation running along its length is, of course, the pea knife. The indentation enables you to balance as many as twenty garden peas (or around a dozen marrowfats) and to get them safely to your mouth without dropping them on the floor.

If you see a knife approximately half an inch long and a quarter of an inch wide, you may be puzzled as to its use. This is, in fact, a doll's house knife which one of the kids has mislaid and is probably frantically looking for.

The long pointed potato knife is an eating implement you come across from time to time. It was specially designed by the Marquis de Sade for the purpose of gouging the eyes out of jacket spuds.

While on the subject of knives, you may like to know that on Christmas Day it is an Edmonds family tradition that lying across the table we have a pair of antique carvers – or Granny and Grandad Edmonds as we call them.

Another unusual heirloom that graces our table from time to time is a ginormous dirk that once belonged to a Scottish ancestor of mine – Rob Roy Edmonds, scourge of the Redcoats. Shaped like a claymore and almost as long, it was used by Rob for tearing apart the flesh of sheep at his al fresco Highland banquets. Och aye, mony's the remark that has been passed on the size of the auld Edmonds's Mutton Dagger.

And now for a word of warning. Would-be comedians are always a pain in the nether regions at dinner parties. You must stamp out any attempt at puerile frivolity.

For instance, if a pig's head is placed on the table for decorative purposes, you can be sure that some 'wit' will attempt to hold a conversation with it, such as: 'I see you've had a face-lift, Noel,' as though he were talking to the host.

Let him see that you are not the slightest bit amused.

Similarly with the person who attempts to use other items of food as props for 'comedy'. I am thinking here of chipolatas, bananas, cucumbers and others of that ilk.

I well remember one infamous occasion where a Great House guest stuck an asparagus up each nostril, turned to the woman sitting next to him, and shouted: 'How's *that* for a walrus, missis?' It nearly ruined the whole evening. Well, you don't expect that sort of behaviour from a bishop.

He must have imbibed too much of Cook's elderflower cordial. You must stamp on this behaviour before it starts.

You must also deal firmly with the sarcastic type who mutters, 'It's a pity the soup wasn't as warm as the wine' or, 'This food is fit for a Prince', then whistles loudly and shouts, 'Here Prince' as if calling for his dog.

In every case, though, diplomacy must be your keyword. When a guest complains that your brown bread is rock hard, point out that he's just attempted to butter and eat a table mat.

Don't let the high jinks get out of hand. Let it be known that playing footsie under the table will not be countenanced. Neither will playing footsie *over* the table. And stress to your guests that playing footsie with their shoes and socks removed can only lead in one direction – athlete's footsie.

We like to serve the food piping hot here at the Great House. This can sometimes cause problems. If your food is equally fiery and one of your diners has a mouthful of food which is proving too hot to swallow, point out that the correct procedure is *not* to spit it back on to his plate (or anyone else's for that matter). The polite method is for him to bring a handkerchief to his mouth and, without drawing undue attention to himself, deposit the offending morsel within its folds.

Care *must* be taken, however, as I recall that in similar

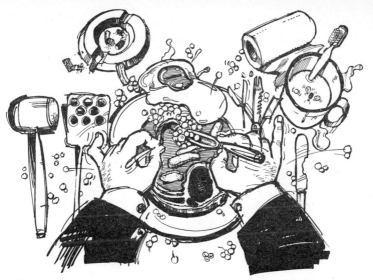

Pea-knife etiquette: The pea knife should be used after stealing the soup spoon, and before asking the lady on your left whether she dyes her moustache

circumstances I once lent my handkerchief to a lady diner who was stricken with a sneezing attack and, to my horror, she walked round for the rest of the evening with a noseful of gristle and turnips.

Now to the thorny question of what to call the afters. In proper circles, like ours, it is always called pudding – never dessert – even when it isn't a pudding. Another point to watch is, no matter how full you are, NEVER loosen the front of your trousers. I once did, and to my everlasting shame, *I* stood up, my trousers *didn't* and everyone in the room fell about laughing and my face went the same shade as the pink underpants I was wearing.

We always have an ample supply of toothpicks – mind you, most Crinkley Bottomers need to have it pointed out to them which end to use. It is also wise to inform them that these are solely to be used for picking their *own* teeth – not anyone else's.

A question I am frequently asked is: what is the correct way to serve the port? Here at Crinkley Bottom we have a well-respected ancient tradition. We usually pass it round by hand. That's once they can get the decanter out of *my* hand of course. Our local undertaker says he's never seen a grip like it in a live person.

On completion of the repast, guests should leave the table along with everyone else and thank the host for his hospitality. The unacceptable thing to do is lean back in your chair, belch loudly and bellow: 'Who's for a takeaway, then?'

Finally, and I mean finally, we come to something which I hope will never arise at your gatherings. That is, what is the correct procedure to follow if the Grim Reaper pays a visit to your table?

For example, if a fishbone should unfortunately lodge in your throat, it is, I need hardly say, extremely impolite to choke to death at the dinner table. The proper course of action is to excuse oneself to one's guests by sign language; slowly rise and effect a graceful and unhurried exit from the dining-room, then go and lie in the nearest rhododendron bushes until the mortal coil is shuffled off. If time permits, a hastily scribbled letter of apology would not go amiss.

So there we are – a few indispensable tips on table etiquette which will stand you in good stead when you next have a bit of a do.

I'd love to share more of my expert knowledge with you but there's someone banging at the door. A lot of men and women on horseback in red jackets – and they've brought their dogs with them.

There's lots of shouting and cries of: 'After the uncouth little idiot with the beard!'

There's no one of that description here. I'll go and let them in.

11. Handling the Servants

Holding a house party isn't all about hard work, at least not for you. There are always those servants to call upon, but they need to be treated in the right way.

The children of Crinkley Bottom frequently ask me, 'How do you handle your servants, Noel?' I look them squarely in the chest, and say, 'Often.' Seriously, though, the Edmonds method of dealing with servants has proved of abiding interest to many people – the TUC, Scotland Yard, Amnesty International, to name but a few.

I don't see why; there's nothing difficult about dealing with servants. Essentially, it boils down to one question: do you rule them with a rod of iron, controlling their every thought, movement and expression on pain of instant dismemberment if they put a foot wrong – or do you take the hard-line approach?

All right, some of you may find this draconian: others'll think it's a bit harsh. But I can assure you, at the end of even the longest, hardest, most taxing house party, I never hear a word of complaint from my servants. So, what's the secret? In a word, earplugs. These take most of the sting out of a servant's resentment; although, I must admit, I've had some pretty menacing notelets over the years.

I command great respect among my staff. The servants all look up to me

How closely you monitor your servants depends upon their capabilities. And in this regard, it pays to hire someone with expertise. Whenever help's needed at the Great House, I always look up the number of Crinkley Bottom's Dial-a-Servant Agency. Then I remember they're not on the phone. Should you find there's no servants agency in your own village, the only solution is to scout around the local restaurants and hotels on a discreet headhunting mission. If you're too busy for this yourself, just get a servant to do it.

Having assembled your cringe of servants, the important thing is to let them know who's the boss, so keep a photo of your mother-in-law handy to show them. Also, impress on them from the outset that, where they and the guests are concerned, you simply won't stand for hob-nobbing. In fact, while they're on duty, they shouldn't eat any kind of biscuits.

How much leeway, then, should servants be allowed at house parties? My own view is that you shouldn't let them get away with anything – and I personally carry out a thorough body search at the end of the evening to ensure they don't. It's not a foolproof method, and I often have to call the young maids back several times to be really sure.

If giving people a dressing down doesn't appeal, however – or if the wife's around – you might prefer to reduce the possibility of your servants taking liberties, and half your best cutlery, by instilling a little loyalty into them.

Here, the mode by which you address them is crucial. Declaiming 'Break open another can of Château Crinkley Bottom '52, Jeeves' or 'Chisel apart some more of Cook's cherry fancies, Rose' may sound very grand, but it's not much good if their names happen to be George and Doris, is it? So make a practice of learning your servants' names. As most servants seem to be called stuff like Dodswell, Wormley, Fuster, Flossie, Brewster, Maisie, Conceptua and Bunion, a sense of humour can help here; as can pinning name badges to their chests.

This doesn't take long. I can get through a dozen waiters in quarter of an hour. The waitresses take a little longer – I usually reckon on two per week – but that's because it's important to check the badge-pin hasn't grazed their delicate flesh anywhere: chest, shoulders, hips, ankles, feet – you can't be too careful, can you? The more worldly waitresses tend to be a bit sceptical of my concern at first, but they're soon reassured, and many even offer to polish the magnifying glass afterwards. It's a nice touch.

Another servant-sensitive area is the question of tipping. Some of you might find it hard to credit, but I frequently tip my servants at house parties – into the punch bowl, mainly. This is not because they've done anything wrong; I just find it improves the flavour. And it's such fun to watch the Crinkley Bottom Body-Building Club wring them out again afterwards, while Pru lies below on the floor with her mouth open.

This, however, is the only occasion when servants are permitted to get soaked at house parties, although even the best of them occasionally flout the rules and have to be reprimanded – I'm delighted to say.

Oh, don't look at me like that. Be honest: what on earth is the point of hiring a bunch of creeping, servile wretches if you can't smack them around now and again? And again. Naturally, you've got to be tasteful about this sort of thing, make sure the welts don't show and the bruises go with their socks, but otherwise, you've got a completely free hand – foot, knee, elbow, and forehead.

Don't get me wrong. I'm not saying you should practise violence at your house party. Good Lord, no! You should practise it well beforehand, so you can get it just right on the night.

And that's what house parties are all about, in essence: getting it just right on the night. The foregoing guidelines should guarantee you a successful relationship with your servants, give or take the odd writ and death threat. But don't think your worries end when your house party does: there's the question of the servants' wages. Like it or not, they're going to want some. And it's no use telling them the cashless society means they don't get paid any more. Even Crinkley Bottom servants aren't that stupid. Well, not all of them.

Therefore, from my unparalleled experience in this field, I've compiled a number of capital excuses which, at the end of the evening, will help keep your wallet in the same condition as your departing guests – green and bloated.

Somewhat Questionable

'If God had intended you to have money, He wouldn't have given it to me first.'

'I'm trying to reduce your risk of being mugged.'

'Call me neurotic, but I just daren't risk you cutting yourself on the edge of a new £5 note.'

'I'm just thinking of the awful wear and tear on your pockets.'

'I would hate to sully our relationship with anything as vulgar as money. How about a conker?'

'Damn! My wallet's jammed in my fist.'

'I was going to offer, but I thought you'd say no.'

'What a coincidence – my rate for counting your money comes to exactly the amount I was going to pay you.'

'Money? Eurgh! You just never know what other people have done with it.'

'I could've sworn you said you were on a sponsored povertyathon.'

Distinctly Dodgy

'If the Queen saw her portrait on those bank notes, I'm sure she wouldn't want me to spread them around.'

'You'd only have the appalling worry of what to spend it on.'

'All those jingling coins and rustling bank notes: the Noise Abatement Society would crucify me.'

'I've always wanted to appear on *Watchdog*.'

'Just consider it my way of protecting you from inflation.'

'I've asked you to do enough already without expecting you to start putting away money.'

'Of course I'll pay you; I just want you to work a year in hand.'

'It's so easy to sprain a muscle lifting those 50p pieces.'

'I thought I'd pay you in kind – in kind of a not-at-all sort of way.'

'Just think of all the tax you won't have to pay.'

Plausible-ish

'I must have overdone it at dinner; I just can't seem to get my hand into my pocket any more.'

'Silly me! I spent your wages on a rack and a couple of electric cattle-prods. I thought you said you wanted *pain*.'

'You'd hate to see me cry.'

'I thought we could agree on a nice round figure – like nought.'

'You mean you're *not* here on a work experience scheme?'

'I'm teaching you how to be treated like royalty. Lesson
one: how not to carry money around with you.'

'Have you no thought for my bank manager's ulcer?'

'I don't understand it: the crane I ordered to prise open
my wallet just hasn't turned up.'

'You broke even: what more do you want?'

'It could be a serious setback to my plans of becoming a
professional tight rich git.'

Only a Tiny Bit Suspicious

'It's impossible to put a price on your services – so I'm
not going to try.'

'Accounting for tax, insurance, inflation, wear and tear
on my floor, and the air you breathed, that's £57.60
you owe me. I'll take a cheque.'

'Money is evil, corrupting and harmful. Look what it did
to me.'

'I get these terrible attacks of openwalletaphobia.'

'Your friends will think you're trying to be posh.'

'This will be valuable experience should you ever get a
job with the BBC.'

'I'm a fervent believer in the redistribution of poverty.'

'It could ruin your chances of ever becoming a
Franciscan monk, you know.'

'It's not that I'm not paying you: it's just that I'm
borrowing it back on a permanent basis.'

'I'm broke.'

12. Handling the Drink

Noel has left me to discourse on the drink at house parties. Why? – No one's had more experience of it than him! No, let's get this right. No one's had more experience of it than he.

Better introduce myself before we go any further: Hal Green. Engaged originally as personal manservant to the great tw— man, then promoted – hah! – to butler, so he could do Hal Green was my valet jokes.

This drink, though. Let's start with the basics. It comes in bottles; it's on the telly more than my boss – and it's more popular; and you don't buy it: you only rent it.

Is it necessary at a house party? Well, it is at the kind of house parties Edmonds throws. Acts as a sort of anaesthetic. Whether you have it at yours is open to question; the question being: would you rather buy in a few crates of the hard stuff, or have your house flipped on its roof and your fingernails removed by berserk guests with white-hot coal-tongs? If you'd prefer the former, read on. If the latter, you shouldn't be copying Edmonds's house parties: you should be serving at them.

– And what marvellous conditions Mr Edmonds's

Crinkleyshire wine: It's not just professional tasters who are advised to spit it out instead of swallowing

servants enjoy! It's hard to imagine a more delightful employer. And fair? That man would give you his last fruit-machine token. Little wonder he's earned the undying respect of the Crinkley Bottom community. What joy he's brought to the villagers' lives with his largesse. He's generous, he's kind, he's amusing, he's –

– gone. Little twerp nearly caught me there. Claimed he'd come back for his tinting-brush. Hah! Scared stiff I'm going to blow the gaff on what goes on up here, that's what's wrong with him. Tales I could tell'd turn your knees green.

Now about that drink. What may I fetch you, sir? Gah! Listen at me. That's Edmonds, that is. Trained me like Pavlov's dog. Someone snaps his fingers; I'm rushing over with my stoop and tray. Three days in hospital with nervous exhaustion after his flaming flamenco evening last May. Hello, what's up now? Someone at the Great House door. Give me a minute, would you . . .

Blasted Crinkley Bottom kids, up to their tricks again. They ring the doorbell, then hang around to ask you which way they should run off. And they've been at that wall again. Aerosols. You've only got to look at the graffiti to know it's the lot from Crinkley Bottom: 'Er . . .', 'Um . . .', 'Der . . .'

This drink: you'll be wanting to know what to get in, won't you? My advice is to pop down to the off-licence, have a look at all the various types and brands and qualities of spirits on offer, and buy them. That's what His Minuteness does – whether he's got a house party on or not.

If it's something special, he visits the Winking Nun and brings back a couple of dozen pints. Usually in his digestive tract. That's the thing with Edmonds: it's quantity, not quality. Except when it comes to his clothes, when it's neither.

Ah, you ask, but what about drinking drivers? Don't be silly; you'd never swallow their shoulders. Got to have a sense of humour, haven't you? Have, if you work for His Shortness. You wouldn't believe what he gets up to with that broken guttering off the stables and a jar of plum –

– crazy about Mr Edmonds, the villagers are. And rightly so. I'd describe him as a truly wonderful man, if it weren't for the fact that 'man' is insufficient a word for him. Minor deity? Angelic presence? Supranatural being? Incomparable –

He's going. Go on, son; shut the door. Stop fondling the handle. Thank you. Habit of his: have I mentioned that? I will. He's bally terrified. Listen; you can hear his teeth chattering. And he's not even got them in today.

What did he want this time? Oh, yes – 'Sorry to interrupt you, Green. Just wondered if I'd left my pin-cushion in here. Not sitting on it, are you? Only your expression seems to suggest you are.' He's a sarky little git. Maybe he was looking for the pin-cushion – he's trying to turn up his boxer shorts so they won't keep tripping him up – but really he's making sure I don't write anything I shouldn't. Worried sick I'll blemish his precious image. Well, he should have thought of that before he bought the scuba suit. Gah! If people only knew what he gets up to. One day, sunshine, one day.

Go on a bit, don't I? Hope he's not charging me for the paper. Time I took another shot at the drink; in particular, the wines. Dangerous ground, this. Do you go for something mysterious and obscure, or something famous and common?

Lentil Brain's wines are all very well known, the most famous being 'Green, I've lost my shoe-lifts' and 'Bunion, I've got a date tonight and I can't find my lady map anywhere.'

If you're into real wines, though, you can't do better than those produced from exclusively local ingredients here in the county of Crinkleyshire. Each village has its own château dedicated to fermenting wines of the finest texture, taste and bouquet. Good stuff? – We're talking up to £4.50 a bottle here!

And there's none of this tramping on the grapes in bare feet, common in foreign parts of other countries abroad. Filthy habit, that. You don't know where the grapes have been, do you? In Crinkleyshire, villagers keep their wellies on to tramp the grapes. And to do most other things in life, come to that.

The choice of Crinkleyshire wines is broader than a motel cleaning lady's mind, and probably more confused, so to give you a guide to the best, I picked ten from the Edmonds house party table, on the basis that if the old skinflint saw fit to unbolt his wallet and buy them, they must be good.

WINE	CHÂTEAU	OFFICIAL DESCRIPTION
Dandelion and Spider	Crinkley Bottom	'fizzy'
Caterpillar and Parsnip	Dangley End	'tarmacky'
Peat and Pesticide	Moistpatch Spa	'gritty'
Spiced Vole	Tinkling-in-the-Bog	'anoraky'
Gooseberry and Hedge	Tinkling-in-the-Bog	'electricky'
Elderflower and Bacon	Throttle St Edmonds	'basset-houndy'
Porridge and Dust	Bluewinkle-by-the-Lake	'roof-racky'
Stoat and Whortleberry	Maggoty Hole	'balloony'

WINE	CHÂTEAU	OFFICIAL DESCRIPTION
Mulled Pram Wheel	Littlewick-on-the-Rise	'fertilizery'
Fern and Hobbit	Nether Scratching	'wellingtonny'

Connoisseurs of Crinkleyshire wine will pardon my excluding Château Bumpkin's End's nettle wine – 'policemanny' – but at house parties you don't want to sit around sucking a dock leaf for ten minutes every time you take a drink, do you?

Don't, incidentally, run away from this with the idea that El Meano is in any way one of these wine experts. (Couldn't bring himself to spit it out, for one thing.) Oh, yes, people often refer to him as a great plonker, but that's not quite what they mean.

I well remember his first – and nearly last – house party, and the embarrassing incident between him and a young Clodaugh Bumpin-Melons. Took DC Hugh Dunnett an hour to convince the little twit that just because it says 'Bristol Cream' on the label, it doesn't mean you can do that with it. And who was it bailed him out afterwards? Not me, that's for sure.

Good Lord! what a racket. Who on earth –? Talk among yourself for a moment, would you . . .

. . . It was the Great House lodger, Dina Lone, yelling and thumping and banging on Edmonds's bedroom door. Gah! In the end, I had to let her out.

Now, about this drink. It raises some rather difficult questions, like: when the direction it takes through your body is quite definitely downwards, how come you wake up next day with a headache? And if lager's so popular, why've they got to keep advertising it all the time? And whose bright idea was it to call a wine 'dry'? And wouldn't it be simpler to make beer twice as strong and use glasses half the size?

But possibly the most common question would-be house party hosts ask is: how do I pour it? Well, if you're anything like Edmonds, the answer's darn quickly. As far as your guests are concerned, though, it's not a question of how, but whether and how often.

Guests here at the Great House tend to be concerned also about how much it's going to cost them. Meanie Mouse's reputation is clearly spreading. Like his stomach. But, to give the little twerp his due, he now makes it a strict and unequivocal rule not to make guests pay for their drinks. He just charges them £50 a go to use the toilet.

You think that's bad? Huh! There's tales I could tell that'd make your toenails curl. There was that time he hired a shark for the Great House swimming-pool, and accidentally dropped the servants' wage packets in –

– all honesty, I fear for the survival of Crinkley Bottom without Mr Edmonds. The village would be as a rose without its petals. His presence serves both as functional lynchpin and decorous ornament. He is a man from whom no honour should be withheld: MBE, Knight of the Garter, OBE –

– Dame of the British Empire. Yes, he's gone, Count Kaleidoscope Hair. Another visitation, 'Just to see how your chapter's coming along, Green, my man. Need any help with the long words – like at and in?' Been thinking up that one all morning, I'll bet. Then he jumps up, has a quick squint over my shoulder, picks up his jar of elbow cream and leaves. No, not his jar of elbow cream and leaves: he picks up his jar of elbow cream, and then he leaves. Well, when I say leaves: he sort of brushes up against the door and quivers his way out in feline slow motion. Got this thing about doorknobs, you see. When he took over the Great House at twenty-one – that was his IQ, not his age – he removed all the upstairs doorhandles, and had Clodaugh Bumpin-Melons model for a new set.

My duties, mercifully, don't take me up there often. Most Great House butlering these days involves fetching and carrying drinks for Micro-Man. You watch; way things are going, it's only a matter of time before I'm replaced by a drip-feed.

He keeps it in the Great House cellar, you know, a dark subterranean room which was officially opened in 1957. Wasn't built then: it just took the family 400 years to find it. If you've not happened upon your own sixteenth-century cellar yet, your best bet is to store the drink in a cool, spacious place that people rarely go, like the loft, or Edmonds's wallet if you can find it.

Hold on. Hear it? That's the Great House's new hi-tec failsafe security system alarm. A Dalmatian puppy. He bought it last week. If dogs take after their owners, it'll be a dachshund before it's three.

Look, I hope you don't think I'm being sour and vindictive about Edmonds. I'm aiming for something much more malevolent than that.

He shouldn't be back for a while. Gone off to find his Reading glasses. No, not reading; Reading. He bought

them in Reading, so he calls them his – no, don't bother.
I didn't think it particularly funny when I suggested it,
but it got him out of the house for a day. Wasting his
time looking for them, anyway, without his day
glasses. And he won't find those without his tri-focals.
Which I've hidden in the garden shed. Under a lawnmower.

Funny thing about house party goers. Sorry; we're
back to the drink. Try to keep up, eh? Other people take
it as read that when they wake up after going to bed on
Saturday night, it'll be Sunday morning. Guests at house
parties like to stay up just to make sure. Most guests are
unable to do this – or anything else involving physical or
mental effort – without help. Alcoholic help, to be
unnecessarily precise. Something warm, full-bodied and
fortifying.

There are numerous beverages which fulfil these
criteria. But here at the Great House, old Corset Guts
likes to give his guests a little punch – and I'm sure they
feel much the same way about him. For once, I agree
with the little tw—

– twinkling star of our village firmament. Mr Edmonds
–or Sir Noel, to be surely only the teensiest bit
presumptuous – is esteemed throughout all three corners
of Crinkley Bottom. His auspicious words are ever in the
villagers' minds; his memory, in their hearts; his name,
on their lips; his image, on their –

– dartboards. Close. Never heard him. The little
twerp's creeping around without his shoes on again.
Saves wear and tear on the carpets – tip number 3,816 in
his *Miserobics Exercise Book*, the second most thumbed

volume in the Edmonds family library next to *How to Be an Idle Git Without Really Trying.*

You do realize that his name's an anagram of Olden Demons, don't you? Spooky, I call it. There's definitely something paranormal about the little toad. Just as we were mentioning his house party punch (remember?), in he sneaks eight seconds behind the smell of his socks, scratches his ankle – without bending – stands on a box to look over my shoulder, and intones, 'Like the bit about the twinkling star, Green. Keep it realistic like that. But, em, discretion, man. I wouldn't want to have to halve the weekly wage packet I pay you once a month, just because you've stupidly revealed something naughty like, shall we say, the ingredients of my secret house party punch, eh, Hal, baby?'

Hah! Tales I could tell about this place, and Rainbow Hair's worried about his punch. What's he take me for, anyway? Tactful, loyal, discreet butler like me, reveal the ingredients of his secret house party punch? Pah! What a suggestion. That's the last thing I'd do.

NOEL'S SECRET HOUSE PARTY PUNCH

12 oz sugar
¾ pint lemon juice
Orange rind curls
2 pints white wine
½ pint pineapple juice
1 pint tea
1 tablespoon Angostura bitters

Rum, port and brandy to taste
Sliced cherries, orange, apple

Heat together the sugar, lemon juice and orange rind.
Stir in the wine and pineapple juice. Pour into a warmed
punch bowl, then add the freshly brewed strained tea,
the bitters and the spirits. Before serving, garnish with
the sliced cherries, orange and apple, and apply for an
explosives licence. (Serves 15.)

(Should anybody require a loyal, friendly and discreet
manservant – you always know where to find me. Try
not to ring on Saturday nights, as we're always a bit
busy then.)

13. Forked Tongues

Conversation is the life-blood of any decent house party. It also, however, brings out the worst in your guests because there is always a great discrepancy between what is said and what is actually *meant*.

This ranges from subtle innuendo to downright hypocrisy and can be hard to distinguish to the untrained ear.

To enable you to do this, here is a guide to typical house party dialogue and what it *really* means.

We simply adore how the room is laid out.
– 'Laid out' as in *dead*.

Of course, we go to all the Buckingham Palace garden parties.
– Who do you think does the washing up?

Your new chef is a real find.
– Where *did* you find him – the Salvation Army soup run?

Your dress is so flowery and spring-like.
– It resembles a well-kept grave.

Your evening-gown has a style of its own.
– It's surprising what you can do with an old potato sack.

House party guests rarely say what they mean. In Crinkley Bottom this is usually because they don't know

They're the sort of clothes that Princess Diana herself would wear.
– To bed.

I have a really soft spot for you.
– The quicksands at Morecambe Bay.

You have done a great deal for the human race.
– By staying out of it.

It's amazing how you really click with all the girls.
– Your false teeth don't fit properly.

Being with you makes me want to jump for joy.
– Off a skyscraper.

There are no flies on you, my dear.
– They all died.

At the Crinkley Bottom Tennis Club, back-handed compliments are common

What a thought-provoking outfit you're wearing, Priscilla.
– Who else would think of wearing court shoes with a donkey jacket.

I do so like a man who clears his dinner plate.
– Not by licking it, though.

I just couldn't wait to be introduced to you.
– I just wanted to see if all the rumours were true.

I bet you have plenty of men at your feet.
– Chiropodists mainly.

You are a gentleman, sir.
– At least, that's what it said on the door you just walked through.

You have looks good enough to be in a film.
– Clingfilm.

I love the way that you give freely of yourself.
– Let's hope your husband doesn't find out.

You have a very open mind.
– And a mouth to match.

It really is a pleasure to meet a self-made man.
– You should've consulted an expert, though.

For a minute I didn't recognize you.
– It was the best sixty seconds I ever spent.

I certainly can't say anything against the food at this party.
– My teeth are glued together.

You don't look yourself this evening.
– It's definitely an improvement.

You make people happy wherever you go.
– So just *go*.

You couldn't fault the drink at this party.
– There isn't enough of it to form a conclusion.

I fear it is incumbent upon His Reverence to absquatulate from the party somewhat prematurely.
– I see the bishop's legless again.

I can't tell you how much we have enjoyed your little soirée.
– That's because we *haven't*.

And a good time was had by all.
– Thank the Lord *that's* over with!.

14. Party Pieces

Party piece: an entertainment presented by guests at an informal domestic gathering.

Sounds simple enough, doesn't it? Don't you believe it. I had the devil's own job trying to get the Crinkley Bottomers to entertain when I began throwing house parties. In fact, the situation became so desperate, I thought I'd have to set the ball rolling myself with a song. And then, unaccountably, everyone was clamouring to have a go.

Just shows that in Crinkley Bottom you never say die. Yes, all right; unless you happen to be my hairdresser. Very amusing. But it's spelt differently: there's a Y in it – a big Y, if you saw her last effort. The myopic Great House gardener parked his lawnmower in front of me waiting for the lights to change; and twenty-nine villagers reported they'd seen the aurora borealis. That tied DC Hugh Dunnett up for two weeks: one day investigating; thirteen working out the spelling.

Just a moment! How've we got on to this subject? My hair's got nothing to do with amusing people at house parties. No, it hasn't. I was about to relate to you the marvellous party-piece performers who've graced the stage here at the Great House. We've had people like

Frank Sinatra, Barbra Streisand, Cliff Richard, Pavarotti. Not them exactly. People like them.

If you yourself are ever to hold a successful house party, it's vital to nurture your guests' budding talents, because, let's be honest, television's awfully lacking in entertainment now I'm not on eight times a week, isn't it? True, CB TV's become more popular since they brought in their new monthly payments scheme – instead of one annual lump sum, viewers can now get paid every month for watching it. But it's not the same as having one of your guests step up to the paraffin microphone and give you a live rendition of 'Danny Boy'. Nowhere near as funny, for one thing.

Sorry, I shouldn't mock. If my own voice weren't such an organ of pure delicate delight, people might make fun of me – once! As it is, well, even my starring role in *Dick Whittington*, our house party Christmas pantomime last June, was rapturously received. It brings a tear to the eye to recall stepping on to the stage and hearing those discerning cries of 'What a Dick!'

There are plenty of things you can do to entertain guests at house parties. Many without risking arrest. Just think of the memorable party pieces local villagers have come up with at the Great House down the years. There's, er, em . . . All right, all right! give me a minute. It's not easy writing and thinking at the same time, you know. Ask Jeffrey Archer. I'm sure I've got something in this drawer . . . Ah, here we are; part of an itinerary listing the imaginative party pieces presented at my last house party, in nostril-offending order:

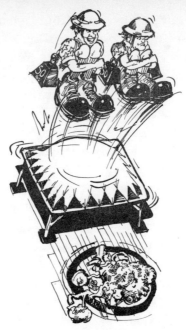

High–altitude Formation Tripe-modelling can lead to fame, fortune and a free bed in a hospital of your choice

1 Mime ventriloquism
2 Finger contortionism
3 Assisted ear-wiggling
4 Synchronized blinking
5 Rhythmic plasticine-thrumming
6 Musical tooth-flicking
7 Tripe-modelling
8 Silent ferret-knotting
9 Long distance magic
10 Underpant yodelling

That took care of the first five minutes, and it provides plenty of exciting ideas. Yes, it does. But it doesn't end there. Do stop moaning.

Many of you will be aware what Prudence Prendergast of the Wool Shop does with her organ – from personal experience, if the rumours are true. But you probably won't know that a splendid display of blindfold axe-juggling is – by overwhelmingly popular demand – presented by the Crinkley Bottom tax inspector Titus A. Ducks, or Stumpy, as we now call him. Fanny Smalls, the village sub-postmistress, is a dab hand at reading tarot cards to tell the villagers' futures, a skill she's adapted from her lifelong habit of doing the same thing with their postcards. And the Crinkley Bottom surgeon's talent for cutting a lady in half with his fifteen-foot buzzsaw never fails to draw gasps of shock and amazement. And I understand he does a rather nifty party piece, too, when he's not at the hospital.

However, it's in the field of singing that Crinkley Bottomer villagers – and, needless to say, I – excel. The average Crinkley Bottomer sings on his way to work, on his way to the barber's, and on his way to the launderette. That's three times a year. Then there's the local church of St Bottom's, and the village football ground, Toepoker Park – both popular venues for dirges. All in all, it's true to say that where fondness for singing's concerned, Crinkley Bottomers are second only to the Welsh and ex-Mafia hitmen.

No one exemplifies this better than the three Frizzett twins, who make up Crinkley Bottom's barbershop quartet. I know, I know, there are only three of them, and it's supposed to be a quartet. I'm not stupidd. But Crinkley Bottom's a small village, and you can't find five good singers just like that.

Nonetheless, the Frizzett twins present their party piece to great acclaim at the Great House, regularly charming guests' ears with such barbershop classics as 'Wash 'n' Go Tell It to the Mountain', 'The Parting's Over', 'How Deep is the Lotion?', 'Bald to be Wild', and 'Shave the Last Bonce for Me'. It's heady stuff, and they even sweep up after themselves. Over your shoes.

Vocal entertainment of another kind comes from Tony Squeak, Crinkley Bottom's solo singer. Tone – short for Tone-deaf, I imagine – began entertaining as an instrumentalist, but developed into an exceptionally mediocre soprano after an accident playing the musical saw. Cut off in his prime, poor girl – I mean, boy. I think.

Lingering with the musical motif, village pig shearer Percy Flage from the bus queue is a very fine house-party fiddler. And I speak for everyone when I say we're all looking forward to the day when he can advance his party piece with the addition of an instrument.

My cousin Quasimodo Edmonds, the twig sorter, was celebrated at 1960s house parties as the only villager able to whistle and hum at the same time. Celebrated, that is, until guests discovered he was whistling through his teeth, and humming through his socks.

With such a tradition of musical entertainment it was inevitable that villagers would develop complementary party pieces, but Mrs Bulstrode's multi-belly dance came as an enormous revelation. Several enormous revelations, to be precise.

Many ingenious ideas for party pieces can be gleaned from the fringe performers at my house parties. Mr Long, the Crinkley Bottom nudist, for instance, thrills guests with a totally unaided fifteen-yard walk along a tight, pencil-thin wire. Admittedly, it might be a shade more thrilling if he raised the wire off the carpet, but at least he has a go. Then there's the Crinkley Bottom alternative comedian, Dai A. D'Eth, who comes out and laughs at the audience. Mustn't forget, either, Crinkley Bottom's alternative animal trainer, Lars R. A. Shins, who balances a seal on a ball by its nose.

Another old trouper is local bus guidance counsellor Sniffer Dimbleby. Sniffer it was, at my 1991 summer house party held in autumn 1992, who, singularly among his village guests, had the steel nerve to volunteer for my human cannonball display. What a man! Bold, fearless, valiant, adventurous: I'd like to shake old Sniffer by the hand. And I will, just as soon as somebody finds it.

Mimickry is popular at the Great House – not just among the staff. The ovoid Lurgy Ogden does farmyard impressions: he comes along smelling like a silage clamp. And village traffic warden Priscilla the Hun is a very fair female impersonator. But for truly professional mimickry, you can't better journalist Maurice Chinking-Jacket's impersonation of a newt. Although many have tried.

Little wonder the Snooty-Burkes of Upper Bottom maintain that, at Great House house parties, it's entertainment with a capital H. And it is, eerily, the Snooty-Burkes' budgie nurse, Flossie Rantzen, who invariably presents the Great House's most cultured party pieces.

Flossie, who knows someone who once listened to a Radio 4 programme, recites from a major work of fiction, such as our village councillors' election manifestos or the Crinkley Bottom bus timetable, then teams up with Illegal Parties graduate Tosh Scrivener to do a monologue. If there's time, and he still has some semblance of control over his central nervous system, Tosh gives us his definitive interpretation of the Crinkley Bottom limerick, entitled 'The Crinkley Bottom Limerick', to wit:

There was a young man from Crinkley Bottom,
. . . .
. . . .
. . . .
He wasn't very interesting at all, really.

As you can imagine, this never fails to elicit long and enthusiastic applause. At least, it would if the typical Crinkley Bottomer were able to clap his hands together more than three times without getting his head caught between them.

Another party piece which goes down better than a Crinkley Bottom DIY shelf unit is that of our inaccurate archer, Dicky Bow. Dicky, short for Robert, has a baffling magic act in which he makes a nice fluffy white rabbit disappear from a sack simply by tapping it twice with his wand and dropping a Rottweiler inside. For an encore, he borrows £1,000 from a member of the audience and makes that vanish, too. It's what's known as his grand illusion, I think. I'll check for sure when the police catch up with him.

Another act popular with the village WI is the Crinkley Bottom body builder. He puts on a display of dancing muscles – well, a dancing muscle; then, with an amazing feat of strength, picks up Clodaugh Bumpin-Melons with a single drink.

Scintillating though these acts sound, you'd be wrong to suppose that all the Great House party pieces are worth emulating. One or two, like Vince the marathon flea-pit diver, hardly come up to scratch at all. Difficult to believe in Crinkley Bottom, isn't it? Yes, it is. In fact, after some party pieces, it can take me twenty minutes to drum up a spontaneous round of applause.

With local butter polisher Anne Teak, this is excusable. How on earth is she expected to put on a half-decent mind-reading spot when there are barely two minds in the whole village worth reading? And both of them belong to livestock.

High-flying Brother Barnabus, the Trapeze Monk, has no such excuse. His virtu-so-so performances, hanging from a bat glued to the Great House chandelier, arouse mixed feelings. Some guests feel he's the most appallingly unentertaining twerp ever to set foot on the planet in the history of mankind. Others don't think he's as good as that.

Undoubtedly not as good as that is Compo Smentis, local daddy-long-legs redesigner and bus queue member (1984–9). I've nothing against siffleurs, as such. If they can't remember the words to a song, whistling along with it's probably the next best thing. But the time Compo forgot his teeth and asked to borrow a set from a member of the audience midway through his piece was definitely not on: it could have been so embarrassing. And what if I'd said no?

The ultimate party piece no-no, however, belongs, if he'll admit ownership, to trainee village idiot Thicky Nobwit. Former ex-policeman Thicky, a part-time thumb whittler, launches his act with a display of solo walking, then demonstrates his equilibrist skill by standing on two legs, both at the same time, without a sandwich. There follows a spot of balancing his head on his shoulders, some joint-nostril breathing, and a coordinated arm-raising display. And the whole act's rounded off with a demonstration of counting backwards with the lights off. Now, I'm not one to cast the first stone at glass houses, but if your guests are anything like mine in Crinkley Bottom, you're going to find this sort of thing just goes right over their heads.

No doubt, having digested the huge array of entertainment feasible at house parties, you'll now want to know how to do it. And some of you might even want to know how to do a party piece. It's impractical to provide instructions for every party piece, owing to the ecological imbalance such a vast amount of additional paper would create, and the fact that the Liszt and Newt opens in fifteen minutes. So I've picked one, exotic dancing, purely at random. I've little personal interest in this art form, and even less experience of it. No, I haven't. When Pru asked for a lift to see the Chippendales, I dropped her off at the antique furniture shop. Therefore, I sought elewdcidation from an adept in the field: a man of the world, broad-minded, acute, someone with all the answers at his fingertips. And who

better than the vicar? Well, any of number of people, to
be honest. But they all wanted paying. So:

```
            The Reverend Dews
            The Vicarage
            St Bottom's Church
            Crinkley Bottom, BC1 0LY
            Tel: Pat. Pending
```

```
N. Edmonds, XDJ
c/o The Liszt and Newt
Public House
Crinkley Bottom, BC1 2XS
```

```
            Date: Later than you think
```

Dear Noel,

Please be seated.

Do you know? when I was first asked to
speak on exotic dancing, I thought to
myself, ha ha, Noel's joking. But, there
being no known precedent for this, I was
forced to reconsider.

There's an old Crinkleyshire saying: a
hero is really a coward with a poor sense
of direction. And do you know? I think
this says it all. For are we not all, in
one sense, this, while, in quite another
sense, really that? Is not the gamekeeper
really the poacher? The chicken, the fox?
The fish, the worm? The trouser-leg, the
ferret? Isn't, in short, the vicar really
the exotic dancer?

True, were I to twitch aside this

cassock and wiggle my rear portions about during morning service, the parishioners of Crinkley Bottom might suffer, shall we say, pulpitations. Least ways, those who remain awake might. But in another sense, isn't this exactly what I'm doing?

While the exotic dancer discards items of clothing to reveal her soft furnishings, so I peel away the layers of doubt to offer a glimpse of heaven. Our respective audiences each require the faith to believe in their hearts that there is something there, unseen, worth hanging around for. And, of course, we both do it to music.

And do you know? Pondering this analogy, it was, so to speak, exposed to me, in a flash, as it were - the midnight skinny-dipping in St Bottom's font, the abandoned support garments in the crypt, the small dripping items found on Gladys Dangley's headstone every Sunday morning. It all became blindingly obvious!

Surely these are the outward representations of an inner desire to strip away the superficial trappings of this world, and get to grips with the divine delights that lie beyond. The underlying logic of it is quite inescapable. The word, indeed, made flesh.

And do you know? I got to thinking some more. And I got to thinking about the wonderful prospects this unavoidable truth presents for the future: for you,

me, mankind, the little church of St
Bottom. Is it, I got to thinking, only a
matter of time before congregations stop
dressing for church, and start
undressing for it? Might nubile young
ladies shimmy out of their Sunday bests
before taking around the collection
plate? Will 'Oh! Come All Ye Faithful'
resound around the belfry while almond-
eyed, butter-lipped, honey-thighed,
peach-bottomed, axle-hipped, soft,
wriggly exotic dancers gyrate on my
organ?
　　Let us pray.

Yours for ever and ever,

Rev

The Reverend Dews

15. You Told Him What?

How to liven up your house party and embarrass your guests with a parent-probing quiz for the kids

Is your mother's least favourite phrase –
a) Happy birthday?
b) Would madam like to try a larger size?
c) Darling, I'm home?
d) Well, that's the last of the gin?
e) Hello, and welcome to *Match of the Day*?

If your father requested your opinion of his dress sense, would you advise him to –
a) come back when he's a fortnight to spare?
b) wear something a bit more modern – like a doublet and hose?
c) stop reading the fashion tips in *Construction Workers' Monthly*?
d) buy something that'll match the beer stains?
e) keep the clothes and get a new body?

Are you proud of your mum for –
a) the way she finds her way home from the pub every night without using her legs?
b) her remarkable ability to convince people she doesn't know your father at parties?
c) her welterweight Lonsdale belt?
d) her taste in children?
e) about five minutes every year?

Does your father's major skill lie in –
a) his unfailing ability to end up behind the world's worst driver every time he takes the car out?
b) his knack of returning from the pub at precisely the right moment to insert his head between the doormat and your mother's rolling-pin?
c) the cultivation of exotic fungi inside a Marks and Spencer's vest?
d) the design and production of the collapsible kitchen shelf?
e) an area presently unknown to mankind?

Do you know that your mother is becoming ever so slightly annoyed when –
a) the wallpaper has fresh toothmarks in it?
b) her fillings melt when she talks?
c) her eyeballs change places and she hires a JCB to tear her hair out?
d) the dog moves its basket on to the roof?
e) she cooks your father's dinner by breathing on it?

Is your father's favourite word –
a) ****?
b) ***!?
c) **!*?
d) *!*!?
e) ****!**!!!****!!!?

Does your mother relax by –
a) standing on her head?
b) standing on your father's head?
c) releasing her grip on the vodka bottle occasionally?

d) visiting the fire station and having her jaws prised apart with a crowbar?

e) inserting pins into a wax doll of the bank manager?

If your father learned he'd become prime minister, would he change –

a) the law on homicide to cover ferrets?

b) the time limit on divorce to about fifteen minutes?

c) his name and move to Bolivia?

d) the country's traffic wardens for go–go dancers?

e) his socks slightly more often?

Does your father irritate your mother most by –

a) forgetting her birthday?

b) forgetting her name?

c) refusing to become a kamikaze pilot?

d) banging on the bathroom door when she's only been in there three hours?

e) breathing?

If your dad were selected for an Olympic event, would it be –

a) the 400 × 1 metre relay?

b) throwing the temper?

c) jumping the shop queue?

d) the 60-metre dash for the pub?

e) the biggest shock since Crinkley Bottom Wonderers won away?

If your mother won a million on the pools, would she spend it on –

a) the way home from the pools company?

b) 250,000 Noel's House Party books?

c) a course of beauty treatment?
d) twenty-four-hour security guards to keep you out of the biscuit tin?
e) a sock transplant for your father?

If your father became a national celebrity, would he be famous for –
a) singing in the bath without the aid of a tune?
b) surviving your mother's cooking?
c) his extensive lack of talent?
d) his campaign to bring back capital punishment for being under eighteen?
e) producing child geniuses?

How did you score?

(a) 0, (b) 20, (c) 1, (d) 5, (e) 10

0–1: Oh, dear. You've got the sort of parents who put the pa in paradox and the ma in enigma. You're oblivious to their habits, ignorant of their ambitions, and confused as to what they get up to in the big wide world when they're not being your daddy and mummy. I hate to interfere here but, at forty-six years of age, don't you think it's about time you found out?

2–3: I know your parents are a bit dodgy and that. But surely it wasn't necessary to write 'Sub Judice' after every question?

4–5: Ah, I think there might have been a slight misunderstanding here. You're supposed to have been answering questions about your mum and dad, not the

British Lions touring team in Thailand. No, no, don't apologize; it's an easy mistake to make. Especially with your parents.

6–10: This isn't so much a score, as the odds against you surviving when your parents find out your answers to this quiz.

11–15: It's hard to know what to say here without being accused of being weirdist. I mean, all parents have their peculiar little ways, and who's to say what's bizarre and twisted and devious and unnatural and – look, let's put it this way: you haven't got an exceptionally tall butler and a cousin called It, have you?

16–20: If what you've revealed about your parents in this quiz bears any relation to the truth, this isn't just a score; it's also your body-to-mouth ratio. Try to avoid zoos; you'll give the pelicans an inferiority complex.

21–25: Fine. No, really. That was fine. There's nothing wrong with exposing your mother's and father's most intimate secrets and mega-embarrassing faults in full and eye-boggling detail. Parents are very understanding about this sort of thing, and I'm sure if you buy them a new car each and lock yourself in your bedroom for the next seventeen years, everything will be fine. Really.

26–30: I hate to break this to you, old bean, but you've got, well, *normal* parents. I'm sorry but there it is. They're ordinary, respectable, sane, sensible, level-headed, conventional and quirk-free. Yes, yes, I know – you're shocked. It must be devastating to discover this sort of thing about your own parents, but at least there's some good news: you don't take after them, or you wouldn't be reading this.

31–35: Congratulations! Such a creditably extensive knowledge of your parents' habits, beliefs and friends deserves to be rewarded with a corresponding raise in pocket money. Tell them you want £150 a week, or you're going to the police.

36–50: Your father's a bit of a puzzle, isn't he? All this hiding in cupboards, avoiding people, refusing to fill in forms, burning his birth certificate, pretending to be someone else on the telephone. Fair enough; he's entitled to behave like a misanthropic, reclusive, paranoid hermit if he wants to, but I honestly can't see why he should be so embarrassed about being called Noel.

51–70: Oh now, come on! I've got a very broad mind – in fact, some people say it's so broad it's thick – but I simply can't believe that your parents are in the habit of doing, well, what you say they're in the habit of doing. For a start, where do they put their – I mean, how can they sort of, you know, without bursting the – no, no, the whole notion's entirely fanciful: it's impractical, and ridiculous, and unbelievable, and have you got any photos?

71–90: Phone your solicitor.

91–110: Phew! You've certainly blown the gaff on your mum and dad here – extravagant, outrageous, zany, lewd, pleasure-loving, decadent, lazy, sycophantic, anarchic, boring, tasteless . . . Hurry up and refill your pen; I can't wait to see how they score on question two.

111–130: This is both your score and, coincidentally, the dimensions in feet of the gag your parents are going to buy you for your next birthday.

131–150: Oh, well done. It's good to come across someone so uninhibited and fearless they can reveal to me the real nitty gritty about their parents. I'm impressed and humbled and touched and I hope you'll soon be able to sit down again and enjoy the rest of this quiz.

151–180: You are to discretion what the M25 is to hedgehogs. You think tact is how carpets are fixed to the floor. And you couldn't keep your lips sealed with a barrel of superglue. And the bad news is that you're verbally incontinent; your mouth stays open longer than Do-It-All; and you neither know nor care what effect your injudicious utterances might have on your poor maligned mother and father. So, how do you fancy being interviewed on the House Party next series?

181–210: Swallow your answers, grow a beard, move to South America.

211–240: Hey! this is really cooking with gas. You clearly have a tremendous mother – caring, sophisticated, youthful-looking. And your dad: well, mere words can't do justice to his boundless charm, generosity, wit and intelligence. You are indeed a very privileged and fortunate child. But I can't help wondering – was it really such a good idea to get your parents to fill in this quiz for you?

16. How to Hold It Outdoors

There can be no denying, holding it outdoors can be very pleasant – there's no better time for doing it than the summer. And here at the Great House we're renowned for our outdoor parties. Did I say renowned? *Revered* would be a better word. Why, I have it on good authority that the Queen herself has slipped in on several occasions wearing a false nose and beard to take notes on how it should be done.

You can't get away from the fact that here at Crinkley Bottom we're very fortunate in our surroundings, nestling, as we do, between the Cotswolds and the Trossachs. Nothing but rolling countryside for as far as the eye can see. Well, that is of course if you've got eyes as bad as our head gardener, Seth Brown – or Drunk and Incapability Brown as he's known in the village.

Brown has done for landscaping what Long John Silver did for trampolining.

You know how Prince Charles talks to his plants? When Brown tries it, they head for the paraquat bottle.

Even the shrubs go into a blind panic when they see him approach – it's a sort of mass wisteria.

I don't know why on earth we employ him really. We don't pay him any wages – I suppose that's something to

Great House gardener Seth Brown: Half man, two-thirds heron's nest

do with it. You can never find him, though: he's always skulking in the potting shed, playing billiards. Last week, he was nowhere in sight. I shouted: 'For goodness' sake man, we're having a barbecue here tonight. Come and shift this unsightly compost heap at once!'

It was only when the compost heap belched, grunted

and shambled off in the opposite direction that I realized I'd been looking at him all the time.

He really is a liability. Talk about lethal. Not only is he acutely myopic, he can't see very well either. When he peers at you through those pebble-lens spectacles of his, it's like looking at two wasps trying to escape from a couple of milk bottles.

Once he gets aboard that sit-on petrol mower of his, you have to have parental guidance just to look at him.

He makes the Texas Chain Saw Massacre look like a Townswomen's Guild beetle drive.

Long after our barbecues are over, we still find our visitors in various parts of the grounds – well, *bits* of them, anyway.

That's when he actually does do the mowing. More often than not, if two people want a decent conversation over the daisies on the lawn, they have to take a pair of stepladders with them. I saw young Nobby Smithers, the YTS schoolboy, there the other day. I said: 'My, you've grown a lot.' He replied: 'I'm on a horse.'

So that's my first piece of advice to you: if you plan to hold a do outdoors, get someone in who's actually capable of looking after the gardens.

Next, find a decent place to site the barbecue. Somewhere adjacent to the Fire Station would be a good idea. It's not a good idea to put it in the centre of a farmer's field. We once placed ours in the middle of a field of maize and ended up with twelve years' supply of popcorn.

Do not site the barbecue under a tree. No one minds eating the odd leaf now and again but accidents can happen. I remember Fanny Duckett, the plumber's wife, saying to me once: 'That lamb was delicious, Mr Edmonds, but the mint sauce tasted a bit funny.'

It was only when we looked up in the tree and saw a barnacle goose looking down that we realized what had happened.

Sometimes – and this is an idea you might like to copy – we like to theme our outdoor occasions.

For instance, if it was a medieval banquet, I would have a big spit in the middle of the lawn. But that's just me – I can't stand the taste of the stuff.

You might like to throw a bring-a-bottle party. I tried that once and they all brought me a bottle of peroxide.

One particular favourite of ours is the authentic Spanish beach party. This is an excellent idea where you empty the septic tank and fill it with seawater; spread a few tons of builders' sand around it; crack open the Sangria, and *hasta la vista*, baby!

For real authenticity, you can bring in a donkey to terrorize and employ a load of beer-bellied England supporters with cropped hair and tattooed nostrils to start a punch-up and then throw up on everybody.

To hold an authentic British beach party, you do exactly the same thing, but don't empty the septic tank first.

The Fair Dinkum Ozzie Barbie is a real doddle. For this, everything is well marinaded in XXXX lager, even the food. As a nice touch, you can stick a few wooden posts in the ground to give the impression it's the *Neighbours* set. Bush hats with corks round are, of course, obligatory, although when Pru last tried this she forgot to take the corks out of the wine bottles first. So do remember to decork!

The Great House barbecue cook makes use of a wide range of local produce – and occasionally even food

I'm often asked: 'How do you go about getting the best from your barbecue?'

I always say it helps tremendously to light it. Try grilling steak on unlit charcoal and your teeth will drop out with old age first. Mind you, once you bite into steak incinerated by Cook they'll drop out anyway, so you just can't win.

When you have the charcoal white hot, you can start to 'barbie' in earnest.

In fact, there's nothing you can't barbecue – coconuts, custard, soups, pork pies, teabags, cornflakes, spaghetti, gerbils – the list is endless.

A particular speciality of Cook's is her succulent

Shrewd siting of the barbecue will ensure your house party is a booming success

barbecued turkey. With a little friendly persuasion on my part, she is willing to share with you this recipe which has been handed down through her family for generations. Or so she says.

Simply take a turkey – preferably a dead one – and shave it all over with a rechargable electric razor. Then cover it with mulberry leaves and chopped tulip bulbs and pour a bottle of dandelion and burdock over it. Wrap it in foil and barbecue over medium heat for three days. At the end of that time, unwrap the foil very carefully and *voilà!* – it's ready to eat. But whatever you do, don't chuck the foil away, as that's the best bit.

She's mustard that woman. The other day, she came up to me and said: 'Master Noel, I've got the shish kebabs.' I said: 'Here's a bottle of kaolin and morph and lay off the bran flakes for a few days.'

She then explained that shish kebabs were a delicacy from the Orient – Leyton Orient, that is – consisting of little bits of dead animals skewered together and grilled on the barbecue. D'you know, she has a real knack for making the most mundane meals sound really delicious.

She serves them in a piquant sauce consisting of Bisto, curried custard and whatever happens to be flying past at the time.

People ask me: 'Do you serve large puddings at your outdoor dos?' I always reply: 'Sit down, we serve anybody.' I've had many a fat lip off that jolly little retort, I can tell you.

I need hardly tell you how popular foreign food has become with the spread of travel abroad. Your guests will doubtless appreciate reminders of their overseas jaunts in the shape of some exotic food.

You'll find that in this respect, you can't go far wrong with seafood. But here again, Cook made her customary cock-up with the octopus. When, machete at the ready, she asked me how to prepare it, I only said to her: 'Just cut off the tentacles.' Well, you've never seen blokes run so fast in all your life.

We had better luck with the grilled spicy sharkmeat. If you have never tried it, I can heartily recommend it. It has only one drawback as far as I can see. Ten minutes after eating it, you have this insatiable desire to leap into the swimming pool and bite someone's leg off. I find it has a slight gamy sort of taste – and so does the sharkmeat.

Perhaps your guests might have a penchant for

Southern fried chicken. It doesn't matter that you don't possess a secret recipe for coating the bird before cooking. I find that if you roll it in a bowlful of Shake'n'Vac, they never notice the difference.

Vegetarians are amply catered for – the Reverend Dews always has a nut roast, but then he shouldn't stand so near the barbecue.

I always think it's a good idea to combine pleasure with fund-raising. I'm a hands-on Charity person, but I always warm them first. But the last do we had got off to an explosive start when I asked Hal Green, the butler, to get some bangers on the barbecue. The next thing I know we're treated to a fireworks display I've not seen the like of before or since.

Aha! I hear you say. Well, *someone* did. All this is fine, and it's all very well little NE banging on about pigging it in the fresh air, but what if it's a typical British summer? i.e. like a typical British winter?

Well, you didn't expect a person of my IQ not to have that one covered, did you? Sid Reckitt to the rescue. He's our local building contractor, who has constructed for me an Authentic Victorian Prandial Gazebo for the purposes of noshing in comfort out of the inclement weather. He assures me that it's the height of good taste – in fact, Fergie has one, I believe.

It's built of old Victorian breeze blocks and has a genuine up-and-over door which once belonged to Queen Victoria herself and which Sid assures me he rescued from the fire at Windsor Castle with his own bare hands.

Admittedly, some people refer to it as a 'garage', but then they're just jealous, aren't they?

At the first sign of rain, we all rush into the gar—, er, the gazebo, which is specially decked out for such functions. As you know, I like to spread around various curios and *objets d'art* for my visitors to remark upon.

Against the walls, we have a collection of ancient samplers. They sample my wine, my brandy, my sherry, in fact anything they can lay their hands on.

If you want a room with a phew, put an unusual animal in it. Our Vietnamese pot-bellied pig always causes comments – mainly ones like: 'I didn't know Bernard Manning was doing the cabaret.'

Inside the gazebo, the English oak banqueting table itself is also a major conversation piece. I don't know the full history, but I believe it once belonged to the Franciscan Friars from the local Crinkley Bottom Abbey. If you look closely you can see where the monks have carved their trademark – 'Monasterum Franciscan Imprintum' – or MFI for short.

I don't know your feelings about taxidermy but I have this big stuffed lion that was given to me by that famous white hunter, my Great-Uncle Clarence. It really is so lifelike standing there in the gazebo. When people ask, 'What is it stuffed with?' I tell them: 'My Great-Uncle Clarence, of course.' It's not, but why spoil a funny story for the sake of authenticity, I always say.

Living statues are also a brilliant source of amusement for any outdoor party. You know the sort of thing I mean. It's where you employ a model to strike a pose and stand immobile for hours on end in various parts of the garden without moving a muscle.

My guests always marvel at them and ask which

agency I got them from. I'll let you into a secret: they're actually Bert Withers, the Crinkley Bottom British Rail station porter; a gas fitter; Elsie the cleaning lady; old Ted Sputum, the barman at the Venus de Milo Arms; and two or three on temporary loan from the local chapel of rest. Well, it saves having to pay someone, doesn't it?

So that's an intimate peep inside my gazebo. I hope it has inspired you to have one built on your estate. There's only one problem. I've got so much stuff in there now, there's no room for any of us to get in there any more, which rather defeats the whole object of it all. Ah well, coffee's served – let's all go and have a stroll around the grounds.

I say. Just a minute. What was that? Was it Pru's stomach doing its impression of the '1812 Overture' or did I hear a rumble of thunder?

Oh dear. Here it comes. It's chucking it down. The Crinkley Bottom monsoon season is upon us again.

Ah, well. There's only one thing for it. Come on, everybody. Swimming cozzies and thermal long johns on. Last one to swim ten lengths of the sunken garden is a cissy!

17. Games

Whether you're indoors or outdoors there's nothing better to help a house party swing than a game.
. . . 'There is nothing like a game! nothing in the world; there is nothing you can name that is anything like a game,' as I remarked once at a house party to Rodgers and Hammerstein. And that, with just a teensy change of words, formed the basis for their blockbusting musical, and my multi-million dollar action for plagiarism against them.

Simply because there is nothing like a game doesn't make it good *per se*, though. There's nothing like a sneeze, a skirting-board, a verruca, or a smack in the mouth with a frozen lobster; and people don't go around immortalizing them in song and dance. Not even Andrew Lloyd-Webber. Yet.

A game, though; that's something special. The house party host feels it as he reclines after dinner on his favourite servant, and watches the evening's guests cavort, cuss and contort their bloated bodies over his latest hilarious diversion. The Germans have a word for it: *Schadenfreude.* It means taking a delight in others' misfortunes. And that, in essence, is what house party games are all about.

You invite these people into your home: they wear out your carpet, your soap, your patience; they devour your food, drain your drink, and gulp your fresh air at no charge whatsoever to themselves. Except a small monetary one. Making them play games is one of the few weapons the house party host has in his armoury with which to get his own back.

From a less vindictive point of view, playing games helps stimulate the heart, providing your esteemed guests with healthy, calorie-busting exercise. And as most of them tend to be fatter than an agoraphobic's dog, they can certainly do with it.

The choice of possible house party games would be endless if it weren't limited by number. I glean ideas for many of mine at Crinkley Bottom's bi-annual Olympic Games, which are held every six years beneath the Crinkley Bottom Olympic flag – five interlinked squares and a hernia – on Nettled Nuttz Field. This, for anyone unfamiliar with Crinkley Bottom – such as the residents themselves – is a triangular area of oval land, bordered on four sides by the motorway bus stop, the one-way cul-de-sac, the underground flyover, and the Great House's north-facing sun lounge. Access is via Joggers' Walk, or the pedestrianized section of the Crinkley Bottom Canal.

The event is attended by shrewd spectators from throughout Crinkleyshire: often all three of them turn up at once. They come to witness some of the finest athletic competition on offer in the Western world. They're invariably disappointed. For, when it comes to sporting awards, Crinkley Bottom Olympians are the kind of athletes who put the trophy in atrophy. Their idea of a major track event is a train leaving Crinkley Bottom Station.

Nonetheless, the game ideas are well worth checking out, because once Crinkley Bottom marathon champion Jocelyn Fore-Position, the fiancé collector, has stumbled into the crucible and ceremonially doused the Olympic flame, the fun, like the rear portions of the lady sprinters, is uncontained.

Proceedings get under way in fine style with the Push of War Contest, Indoor Kite Flying, Catching the Javelin, Putting the Gravel, and the Widest Long Jump (Backwards-in-a-Hairnet) Competition.

Next comes the adrenalin-charged Women's 400 Metres, where sprightly young females bound around the track then race to be first to tug their leotards out of their bottoms. This is followed by the High Jump, in which Crusher Nuttz, the tripe-modeller, invariably gets lapped; the Boxing Competition, which customarily ends with referee and trouser mechanic Ygor Blimey disqualifying the competitors for fighting; and the 100 Metres Sprint, where it's always a fair bet that all-round athlete Ivor Groin-Strain will lose his way ninety metres from the tape.

The Uphill Skiing concludes the Games in typically exciting fashion, with Twiggy Rushton, putty-medal favourite and transport-café survivor, racing against the clock to get his pants on over his skis.

Giggle-stuffed though they are, such games may not suit your house party. Your guests might be too aged, or infirm, or unathletically inclined. Or you might even like

149

some of them. No sweat; Crinkley Bottom has a farmer's wellyful of traditional old folk games, many of them not involving sheep, which have been played down the ages and immortalized in various local historical documents: residents' diaries, parish records, police charge sheets. Ancient they may be, but each is in perfect working order. Sometimes I get guests at the Great House to have a go at them. Other times, I just pull the legs off millipedes.

Cow-pat Trampolining is perhaps the best known of these games. You've probably smelt it yourself. It's popular, amusing and enormous fun. Unless you happen to be playing it, that is. Pig-trough Surfing, too, is a hoot: villagers strip down to their spring clothes, and first one in's a stinker.

An ancient village pervers— I mean, diversion that I must go into is the superior and immensely skilful game of Goat Guessing. For this my Uncle, Professor Merrilegs Edmonds, the history forecaster, is unroped and sent out at dawn to paint lines on the Great House's quoits lawn, in order to divide it into squares. On his return, he generally has to be clipped around the hearing-aid, pointed back in the direction he came, and told not to use green paint.

Step 2 entails releasing one of the Great House's battery goats from their annexe in the hamster cage. It's crucial here to ensure that the chosen goat has been on a pure silage diet for forty-eight hours beforehand.

Immediately prior to the house party's commencement, my great-niece Vanity, the fearophobic, takes the goat out on to the quoits lawn – leading rather than driving is a shrewd idea here, by the way: or use a cork – and guests play the game by gathering at the Great House windows and guessing which square of lawn the goat will unburden itself in. A subtle if less exact variation of the game involves silage-feeding the goat for ninety-six hours, then guessing which square it won't unburden itself in.

Not all old Crinkley Bottom games are like Goat Guessing. Some are pretty tasteless. Yes, really. In Crinkley Bottom – can you believe it! But you wouldn't want anything like that at your house party. No, you wouldn't. Take it from me. – That's the title of one of the more mentionable ones, coincidentally. See what I mean? You'd be much better advised to stick to the respectable stuff, like Spinning the Chamberpot, Musical Trousers, and Hurdling Clodaugh Bumpin-Melons.

Or you may prefer intellectual pursuits. OK, it's unlikely, if you're reading a book like this, but bear with me; you might recognize the odd word or two. Top of the list comes the game devised and practised by Jez Oik, cruet lagger and campaigner for VAT on Scottish football results. In the game, Jez, or Jeremiah for short, starts out with a bundle of envelopes, each bearing a different villager's name and address. When he's sure nobody's looking, he hides them singly, at random, in secret, unusual or inaccessible locations around Crinkley Bottom. This done, the residents have to chase around, hunting all over the village until they find the envelope with their own name and address on it. The game, albeit practised almost daily in Crinkley Bottom, has no name as such; although the Post Office call it their postal round.

At house parties where the guests are not quite so adventurous, I send Hal Green, the Great House butler and assassin-in-waiting, up to the rummage room for Great-Uncle Ebeneezer's two-piece jigsaw. It used to be a one-piece jigsaw, but Eb got angry and broke it when he found he couldn't do it.

Which brings me to Blindfold Cribbage, a legendary local card game played at all Great-Uncle Ebeneezer's house parties. Ah yes! old Eb's Blindfold Cribbage evenings: even I, a mere sapling, can recall those long hours of concentration and suspense, exhaustion and confusion, despair and delight. And that was just picking the cards up after he'd shuffled them.

They don't invent games like that any more. The best modern Crinkley Bottom game occurs when the Great House kitchen staff serve up a particularly undercooked dinner, and the guests chase the steak around the bedrooms before they're able to eat.

Turnip Baiting and Pin the Bomb on the Bagpiper are also recent developments, as is the exclusively Crinkley Bottom pastime of Spot the Brain Cell, a game instigated by Lady Phillippa Yoyo-Bloomers, the cagoule weaver and elbow critic, in 1983, and still not won to this day.

Games in the Great House swimming pool, perennially popular – except when it's wet – have fallen into temporary disfavour, owing to guests misunderstanding the sign in the garden, which says 'Please Do Not Go in the Pool'.

While we're on the subject, it's worthwhile paying tribute to those intrepid souls who take part in your games, for without them your house party can be as

152

dead as a deaf hedgehog, and as short as a fire-eater's moustache.

Here at the Great House, we've nailed up a brass-plated gold plaque in honour of guests who've excelled themselves at house party games over the years. The names trip off the tongue with throat-clotting piquancy: Twirker Birmingham, bidet coach; T. Splodge Pretty-Boycott, inventor of the waterproof carpet slipper; trainee village idiot Thicky Nobwit, who's so stupid he once cut himself on a sharp bend; Dizzy-Ann Moore-Onique, the famous anonymist, who hates people who keep trying to talk while she's interrupting; and Tinkler Reed, who would have made a great Crinkley Bottom athlete if only he hadn't failed to break his leg as a schoolboy.

Installing plaques is maybe a rather posh way of honouring house party gamesters. Well, for you it is. So you may care to consider alternative methods, such as prize-giving.

I'm all in favour of prizes. They're memorable, easy, exciting. It's the giving bit that worries me. I'm a gnome man, myself. Watch it! I sell them, rather than give them away. It's much more ecognomeical.

Great-Uncle Ebeneezer had no such inhibitions. In his house party days he may only have been five-feet-zippo with his hat on, but that man had a big heart. Not for nothing was Eb known as the man who put the mouse in magnanimous. And if you're the king of tw— host who's into actually giving away prizes, you incorrigible old b— benefactor you, you can't do better than the prizes Eb distributed.

First prize was always a course of bossa nova lessons

at the Crinkley Bottom Dance Academy, and a free crutch. A genuine leather-covered cow made up the runners-up prizes, along with a signed copy of Seth Brown the gardener's *Brief History of Thyme*, a gerbil muzzle, and a medium tin of the Crinkley Bottom Repertory Company's Theatrical Toffee.

Those were the great days of house parties, when inflation was something you did to balloons, and thrift was a noise polite ladies made when they sneezed. All different now. But that doesn't mean guests can't enjoy themselves. They can. They do. Damnit. – Which brings us conveniently back to house party games.

The games I've mentioned so far will prevent guests who are enjoying themselves having a good time while they do so. The games I'm about to mention will prevent guests actually enjoying themselves in the first place. Or anywhere else, for that matter. One word of warning – use them with care; there might be members of Amnesty International present.

Potty Relay

Victims – sorry, guests – are arranged into teams, each of which is provided with four sturdy plant-pots, or four saucepans your house party cook has failed to burn a hole in. Balancing on his four pots, player one in each team races to the opposite end of the room, touches the wall, and returns to his team, whereupon player two takes over the pots, and sets off himself.

If any player touches the floor or uses anything as an

additional balancing aid, he must return to his team and start again. The winner is the first team to get all its players safely back from the opposite wall. An interesting variation is to start each team from a different wall in the room.

Remote-controlled Robots

Each team of house party gamesters elects a player to be its robot. The robot is blindfolded, spun three times and directed via his team's cries through an obstacle course of cushions, chairs, boxes, newspaper stacks, magazine racks, heaped pullovers and vases – not the Ming one, eh? – to the futuristic robot-recharging zone, namely a pair of wellington boots, into which he must place his feet without use of the hands.

If there's insufficient space for each team to have its own obstacle course, or if you're short on wellies, set the robots off along the same course one at a time, and time them with a stopwatch, adding ten seconds for each obstacle touched.

House Hunting

Teams are given separate lists of objects, and have to hunt around the house to find them. The lists comprise simple, ordinary items, the sort of things you'd find lying around the Great House: a gentleman's corset, a bucket of hair dye, a chambermaid's begging bowl, toupée glue, a blood-stained butler, and so forth. The winning team is the one which has discovered most objects within a time limit of fifteen minutes. Best played in someone else's house.

Losing Your Marbles

Players in each team queue up behind player one, who holds a dish of five marbles. When the game starts, the dish must be passed, alternately between the legs and over the head, down to the final player, who then runs to the front and begins the passing process over again. Any marbles which fall off must be replaced before the dish can continue on its journey. The team which ends up with player one at the back of the line, holding the dish of marbles, wins.

Cheek to Cheek

A drink in a plastic beaker is supported between the right cheek of player one and the left cheek of player two. They then race against other pairs over a course which incorporates plenty of climbing and twisting obstacles. The pairs must return to the start if they use their hands, or spill more than half the drink. For goodness' sake, don't use whisky.

*   *   *

Two Up

Teams are chosen, and each lined up behind the back of a chair over which a pillow-case has been hung. (To save washing afterwards, a bin-liner or a shopping-bag may be used, instead.) The pillow-case has been stocked with numerous pairs of objects: two socks, pen, walnuts, golf balls, matchboxes, toupées, rubber spiders, used teabags, slices of buttered toast – be as disgusting as only you know how; nothing sharp, though.

Player one in each team puts on a blindfold, and has to dig around in his pillow-case, removing one object at a time, until he finds two which match. His team may offer advice by shouting things like 'What a plonker' if he hasn't found two matching objects, or 'What a pair!' if he has.

Having acquired his pair, player one places the blindfold on player two, who starts searching for his own pair, and so on down the line. The first team to equip all its players with matching objects wins.

Puff Balls

Players place a drinking-straw in their mouths, and gather around a table. A table-tennis ball is dropped on to the table by a referee. Each player then blows through his straw to keep the ball away from him. A player is disqualified when the ball is adjudged to have been blown off over his section of table: the ref's decision is final here, even though it'll probably be wrong. The winning team is the one with most players left in the game at the end of a designated time.

157

Grasshopper Race

Each team's players form a queue behind player one.
They squat, with their hands on the shoulders of the
player in front of them, thus becoming a grasshopper.
On the word go, the members of each grasshopper race
to a finishing-line by hopping in unison. If any player's
hands become dislodged from the shoulders of the player
in front, his entire grasshopper is disqualified.

Progress is made much easier if one player per team is
designated to act as coach and call out a rhythm for his
grasshopper. But then, you don't have to tell them that,
do you?

Apple Turnover

Teams line up, alternately male and female, shoulder to
shoulder. Player one places an apple under his chin, and
turns to player two. Without use of hands, she has to take
the apple from him so that it ends up beneath her own chin.
She then turns to player three, who repeats the procedure.

If the apple falls, the team must start all over again. The
first team to pass the apple to the end of its line wins. Play
this game only after dinner, or some fool will eat the apple.

*   *   *

The Lord of Crinkley Bottom

Each team selects one player to be the Lord, and two more – male and female – to be his valets. The Lords discard an equal amount of non-essential clothing: jackets, pullovers, ties, shirts, shoes – trousers, in some cases: and the pairs of valets race against one another to re-dress their Lords. What makes this really tricky is that the valets must keep their left hands behind their backs and manoeuvre the clothes with only their right hands.

The Mating Game

This is a game for equal numbers of male and female players. Surplus players must sit it out, so lock up the cocktail cabinet. The names of Crinkley Bottom Zoo animals (for instance, mules, cows, cats, beetles, a timeshare elephant) are written on as many slips of paper as there are male players, duplicated, and placed in bucket one. The copies are placed in bucket two. The male and female players each take one slip of paper from buckets one and two respectively, and become the animal which is written on the slip.

The players are now informed that there's been a mass breakout from the Crinkley Bottom Zoo. Grandmother is sent to bed, and the lights are turned out. The players get down on all fours, and, by making appropriate animal noises, try to find their mates – the players of the opposite gender with the same animal written on their slips of paper. The winning team is the one with most players paired up at the end of a designated time. For decency's sake, make it less than ten minutes.

Crinkley Squash

Player one goes off and hides. The others, acting individually, search for him. As each player discovers where player one is hiding, he hides along with him, until everyone but the final player is crammed, sardine-like, into the hiding place. The remaining player then has to go off and hide, and the game begins over again.

Pass It On

The players in each team line up shoulder to shoulder. Before player one stand an empty bucket and a washing-up bowl full of ordinary household objects: old fish, beakers of water, wet loofahs, brassières, fried eggs, toenail clippings, cucumbers – you know, really tasteful stuff. The object-ive of the game is for the players to pass the items from the bowl down their line in front of them, then pass the items back up their line behind them. There is no limit to how many items may be in transit at any particular moment.

As each item is returned to player one, he drops it into the bucket. The winner is the first team to transfer all the items from the bowl into the bucket. For optimum confusion, arrange it so that the number of items in each washing-up bowl is about double the number of players in each team. It also helps if the buckets aren't quite large enough to hold all the items from the washing-up bowl.

Reflections

Players from all teams disperse around the room or garden, and face the instructor, who performs a series of asymmetrical movements: hopping, winking, windmilling one arm backwards and the other forwards, and so on. Within a period of three seconds, the players have to perform the mirror image of the movement made by the instructor. For instance, if the instructor raises his left arm and spins clockwise, the players must raise their right arms and spin anticlockwise.

Adjudicators disqualify players who get it wrong or take too long. The winning team is the one with most players left after a designated time.

Silhouettes

A bed-sheet is hung or held across part of the room, and a lamp shone on to it from a safe distance behind. The room lights are doused. Team one's players retreat behind the sheet, and cross it individually in postures and clothing designed to confuse the players of team two, who are sitting in front of the sheet, writing down on a score card the names of the players they think they're seeing.

When all team one's players have crossed, team two takes its turn behind the sheet. The winning team is the one to have guessed more silhouettes correctly when the score cards are checked at the end of the game.

It's in Your Pocket

The host holds up two identical envelopes early in the house party, and announces that one contains a one-way ticket out of Dangley End; the other, a Crinkley Bottom Wonderers season ticket. The envelopes, he says, will be secretly circulated throughout the evening. The guest who winds up with the first envelope at the end of the house party will receive a prize; the guest with the second envelope will have to pay a forfeit, such as drinking a glass of fizzy water while standing on his head, or having a bowl of jelly poured down his underpants.

An unidentified helper begins circulating the envelopes by slipping them into the pockets of two unsuspecting guests, then whispering 'It's in your pocket.' The guests must decide whether to keep the envelope, or pass it on in the same manner they received it. If any guest is caught in the act of passing the envelope, he, too, must pay the forfeit.

PRIZE IDEAS

Noel's Most Popular Prize House Party Gnomes – and the Prices Guests Get Charged for Them

The Crinkley Bottom soldier gnome (yellow with broken arms) £14.19

The Crinkley Bottom Observer gnome (red with a puzzled frown) £0.30

The Crinkley Bottom anarchist gnome (green and reign-resistant) £34

The incredible Crinkley Bottom flying gnome (travels up to forty feet through the air – or more, depending on how far you throw it) £13.99

The Crinkley Bottom hand-painted gnome £8 (extra £5 to have the rest of its body painted)

The Pitz Cinema gnome (features out of focus) £4.50

The Liszt and Newt regular gnome (fragile head, legless) £9

The Noel gnome (small and full of little cracks) £15.50

The Cousin Peaches Edmonds gnome (goes with the pansies) £12.69

The Prudence Prendergast gnome (organ needs touching up) £25

The Great House servant gnome (short) £7.50

The Clodaugh Bumpin-Melons gnome (booby prize) £42.26.32

18. Gotchas!

Before we go any further, I have a confession to make. This book has a secret transmitter in the spine and I can hear everything you say. Not only that; there's a mini-camera pointing straight at you. See this question mark? Look closely at the dot below the curly bit. You'll see it's not actually a full stop; it's the latest in micro-technology, and I'm looking right up your nose at this very minute. Not a pretty sight: you couldn't just move the book a wee bit to the right, could you? That's better.

Yes, at this very second, YOU are on NTV. Isn't science wonderful? Here am I in the communications control-room at the Great House, spying with my electronic eye on people all around the country who've bought a copy of this book, and tuning in willy-nilly to see what they're up to. I'll just zoom in on someone at random.

Good heavens! Mrs Lily Battersby of Luton, you look different with your teeth out and your curlers in. Funny place to put curlers. And who's that with you? He looks suspiciously unlike Omar Sharif. From the way he's just dived under the bed, I'd say he looks more like the lodger.

And here's a nice surprise for you – Mr Ron

Thistlethwaite of Todmorden. Well, pull them up quickly – you shouldn't have been reading a book like this in there in the first place. What a cheek!

Oh, I do enjoy this. And now we have established contact, dear readers, I want you all to do something for me. Put the book on your lap. That's it. Now all smile at the camera, give a big wave and after the count of three shout: 'We love little Noel!' One, two, three.

Ha ha – GOTCHA! There isn't really a camera in the full stop. But come on, admit it – I had you going for a bit there, didn't I? There *could've* been a hidden lens – how else do you think we get our victims? It's not that *I* approve of making folk look foolish, you understand. I leave that sort of thing to the people who make carpet warehouse commercials and ginger toupées. I don't actually approve of gotchas at all. It's the powers that be on the telly who make me do these things. Yes, it is. I can't stand people who make fun at other people's expense. Take the Gunge Tank, for example. I'm glad to say that wasn't *my* idea, because I thoroughly disapprove of cheap laughs. They really had to twist my arm to put it in the show – until the producer pointed out to me that it gets a laugh and, well, it's *cheap*.

It's not as if we force people to have gunge poured all over their heads, although admittedly we did tell Paul Daniels it would make his hair grow again, and we might have given Mary Whitehouse the impression it was a bus shelter, but that's not the point.

Be honest: if we can't have a real good laugh at other people's misfortunes, why have a royal family in the first place?

165

They've caught even me out in the Gunge Tank. Who was the one who laughed loudest as I sat there covered from head to foot in the green, slimy goo? Why, *me* of course. You've got to show you can take it as well as give it, as I said to the producer just before I handed him his cards.

All this talk about gungeing people should have given you the urge to do it at your own house party. You won't be able to afford a good quality Gunge Tank and revolving stage – even the BBC can't – but never fear; a couple of plastic buckets over the door work just as well. (We did try it with steel buckets, but we kept getting visits from Miss Marple.)

All you need now is the Top Secret Gunge Recipe which the DG of the BBC keeps locked in his special thief-proof galvanized steel safe for security reasons. Good job he leaves the key on top.

TOP SECRET GUNGE RECIPE

Steep 3 sacks of horse manure in a barrel of rainwater for 6 weeks. Remove sacks and to the liquid add:
1 bucket of pigswill; 3 dozen rotten eggs (free range); 6 large cartons of yoghurt, shaken; 16 dead jellyfish; some old toenail cuttings; the bruised skin of a pre-war rice pudding; $\frac{1}{2}$ a dozen sheep's eyeballs, diced; 1 pint of lager; a bucket of Crinkley Bottom pond sludge; a *Crinkley Bottom Observer* (white-print edition); the contents of a spittoon, thickened if necessary; 6 cubes of yellow jelly; 3 well-sucked bus tickets to Dangley End (very rare, these); a crate of black squidgy bananas – or a Luton Town supporter; a peck of dung beetles, finely

ground; 1 gallon of mushy peas; ½ lb of goosegrease; a tin of Germolene; 12 quarts of cold baked beans; 1 hedgehog, mashed; 10 bags of pork scratchings; ½ a teaspoon of ear wax – left one; a large chunk of ripe Stilton, gone green; a bag of monkey nuts; the juice of a wombat; 6 oz of mulled belly button fluff; 12 kilos of donkey droppings, steaming; 7 dessertspoons of that yucky slimy stuff you find at the bottom of plugholes; a medium wellingtonful of liquidized turkey giblets – bootiful; 2 cubes of frozen Crinkley Bottom anti-freeze; 3 verrucas – in blossom; 2 buckets of spiders' legs; and a pinch of parsley (optional).

Regular diners at the Great House will have spotted that this is also the recipe for Cook's Crinkley Bottom hot-pot. Well, those who are still conscious will have.

Gungeing isn't the only way to give guests your own equivalent of a gotcha. There are many tried and tested traditional Crinkley Bottom practical jokes. Not that I approve, I hasten to add.

You wouldn't catch me doing anything so puerile as hiding mousetraps in the Great House's house party bran tub or putting senna pods in the apple-bobbing bucket. Good Lord, no! I prefer something much more cunning. What on earth is the use of putting mustard in the custard and rubber fried eggs on the breakfast table when no one would notice the difference anyway?

I will admit that I once laced Maisie the maid's bed with itching powder, but for the life of me I could not work out why it was Bunion the under-butler who came downstairs scratching like mad in the morning.

Preparing the gunge requires a sharp eye and a firm hand –
and several other, even stranger ingredients

Great-Uncle Ebeneezer Edmonds was the real joker in
our family. He'd drop a viper down your trousers as
soon as look at you, and he filled all the bathrooms with
exploding loofahs. Sometimes he'd leave a dead carthorse
in someone's bed so that when they complained he could
say it was just a nightmare – but it was all good completely
harmless fun, of course. He wouldn't do anything
malicious. Unless you count the time when he superglued

half a crown to the dance floor at the New Year's Eve Ball and gave three villagers a hernia trying to pick it up.

But there was no real harm in the man – he just liked a good laugh. OK, so DC Hugh Dunnett took him in for questioning after he wired up the front doorknocker to the mains and invited the local Jehovah's Witnesses round for a discussion, but I expect they all had a jolly good laugh about it as well. I know the judge who sent him down for six years did.

Good job my guests enjoy a prank. I think that to play a practical joke on house party goers, you have to get them in the right frame of mind. The technical term for it is legless. Get them drunk and dump them in the stocks I say – Cook's chicken or hambone stock if possible; they still come out smelling the same.

Watch their faces when the local bobby comes round and takes them into custody for being drunk in charge of a smirk; or for being the owner of a slight stoop without a licence, or having possession of a pair of fancy brogues with intent to do serious walking. Imagine their relief after they've spent six nights in the clink only to find out it's all been a jape.

A tried and tested practical gotcha is the old fool's errand. You know – where you send someone out to the hardware store for some ridiculous object or other such as a left-handed cucumber corer, a sponge watering-can, a glass carpet beater, a bucket of steam, a long wait, a rubber poker, or a skirting-board ladder. Trouble is, Crinkley Bottom being what it is, they manage to buy ten, and we now have umpteen roomsful of the things!

Sometimes at the Great House we go to elaborate

lengths for the sake of a good laugh. At massive expense – well, £3.50 and all the gin she can drink – we hire an expert from the BBC Makeup Department, or Brucie's Embalmers, as they are more familiarly known. In the middle of the night, she creeps into the bedroom of a married couple whom we've singled out as the 'hit', and with the aid of spirit gum, whiskers, wigs and felt-tip pens, transforms the couple to look like well-known celebrities. The likeness is absolutely uncanny. You can picture the wife's astonishment when she wakes up the next morning next to Terry Wogan. Even worse is the husband's sheer terror when he looks across the pillow and sees Jimmy Hill staring back at him!

Now everybody knows I haven't got a sadistic streak – not unless you count the rather attractive blond one that goes through my dainty coiffure – but if you want a real hoot at your next house party, tell just one couple it's a theme party – such as a Jocky Wilson lookalike evening. You'll fall about when, to the amazement of the rest of your visitors, they walk through the door with no teeth in and a cushion up the front of the tartan darts shirt, shouting: 'One hundred and eighty!'

I know what you're thinking. You're thinking it's all very well me going on about taking the mickey out of people, but not everybody likes it. When's he going to give us one to make someone look a *right* twonk? So for the seriously humanely impaired among you, here's a genuine gotcha straight out of Great-Uncle Ebeneezer's *Manual of Greatest Gotchas* (volume 694).

To set it up, you get two identical soup bowls (but

not your best ones), and hold one over a lighted candle until the bottom is all sooty and black.

Fill both bowls with water and give the sooty one to some unsuspecting party. Tell him the idea of the 'game' is that he has to look into your eyes all the time, while holding the soup bowl with one hand at waist height, and copy every move you make as though hypnotized.

Make out it's an intelligence test on how speedily and accurately he can follow your actions. Then, in quick succession, wink, blink, nod and shake your head; then 'baptize' yourself in the water.

Circle the rim of the bowl very slowly with a finger and wipe your brow with your hand. This is where it gets good. I can hardly wait to tell you – my little legs are quivering with condensation.

Still fixing your eyes on his, rub the bottom of the bowl with your right hand. Raise your hand quickly to your face and rub each cheek. He will do likewise, covering his face – tee hee – with soot. Do the same and draw a squiggle on your forehead or a line down your nose and so on until – oh, the joy – his face is black all over and your guests are rolling with laughter on the floor.

That's all there is to it. It's a gotcha we play all the time here at the Great House. In fact, I've just done it to one poor idiot and everybody here's in hysterics. I can't understand it, though. His face is pristine white – not a smudge in sight. What on earth could have . . . Oh dear. Yes. OK, smartypants, so I goofed it up. *I* had the sooty bowl and gave him the clean one. So what? Don't worry. I've told you before. I can take a joke. They don't call me Equanimous Edmonds for nothing. Well, what are they standing there for, grinning like a load of gibbering baboons? Anyone'd think they'd never seen anyone with soot all over his face before. Go on, get out, the lot of you! Clear off, you freeloading layabouts, before I lose my sense of humour! And pass me the cat while I kick it . . . Blooming gotchas!

Good riddance. Now, time to get back to planning my next house party . . . I wonder where Uncle Ebeneezer left his sack of exploding loofahs . . . ?

19. Good Lord – Is That the Date?

How to get rid of those unwanted guests

You know the feeling. It's that time of night which is the high spot of any house party. When it's *finished.*

Your head is throbbing with all that inane chatter, your cheeks are aching from holding a false smile all evening and you've a sharp pain in the end of your index finger from working out on your pocket calculator how much it's all cost.

But there's just one problem. Most of your guests took the subtle hint when you slipped into your jim-jams and hung by your toes from the rafters, making a loud snoring noise and doing a passable impression of a bat. But have you ever noticed that at any house party there is always some thoughtless person prepared to abuse the hospitality of the host by lingering around long after all the other guests have taken their carriages home?

I should know, having been there at the end of other people's house parties and *seen* these inconsiderate people myself. They drape themselves like clingfilm over your sofa and no amount of looking at your watch, or even the calendar, has any effect in persuading them that they have far outstayed their welcome. I know what I'm talking about. I've been sitting at the side of these laggards when they do it.

Shifting your guests: Not so much a goodbye, as a thirteen-year prison sentence

Like the man who gets invited to all the best houses – *once* – these people are total boors and ought not to be tolerated, as they will spoil any occasion with their thoughtless behaviour.

Indeed, I well remember one country soirée where a particular guest dallied so long into the wee small hours that his understandably frustrated host threw him by the seat of the trousers bodily into a holly bush by the front door.

So if you are plagued by someone who appears to be superglued to your chaise-longue, fear not. Based on long years of practical experience of house party throwing, here are a number of choice subterfuges which I guarantee will have them vacating the premises faster than snow off a hot shovel.

First of all, let me make it perfectly clear that I think it would be totally reprehensible for any host to make use for his own purposes of a guest's particular personal phobia – like fear of rabid dogs. Nevertheless, here's a cracker that never fails – especially on people with a fear of rabid dogs.

Wait until the unwanted guest is looking in the other direction, then surreptitiously slip your pet pooch a handful of Alka Seltzers. Wait a few seconds, and as the foam slides down the dog's jowls, causally remark: 'Of course, we never bothered to have Binkie quarantined after we smuggled him back in the boot of the car from Morocco.'

Amazingly simple it may be, but at this point they suddenly remember they've left the chip pan on at home and their car tyres leave scorch marks on your drive.

This is what I call my psychological approach. Although I draw the line at physically injuring dilatory ditherers, I don't mind giving them the odd electric shock if it gets shot of them before dawn. To this end I have devised an ingenious and reasonably cheap gismo involving a time switch and two pieces of electrical wire. What you do is wire the chair up to the mains and set the apparatus to the time you desire the person to depart, then, as the voltage lifts him into the air, you rise simultaneously and say sweetly, '*Must* you leave so soon?'

Prime the butler to propel them out through the door before they have time to recover. It helps to spill your drink on their feet beforehand as well, but I would only do this as a last resort. Have you seen the price of booze these days?

And, talking of horror, devotees of this genre will

doubtless enjoy the next one, which is for those of a theatrical inclination. With a pair of scissors, carefully cut some hair off the back of your head (or someone else's head if you happen to be follicularly disadvantaged), glue these to your hands and cheeks, then as you bend down to hand the visitor a cup of tea, remark, 'I see it's a full moon tonight.'

Accompanied by a sickly leer and perhaps a slight lolling of the tongue, this is particularly effective on little old ladies. And it saves them a fortune in laxatives.

You don't *have* to be so brutal. Only if you enjoy it, of course, but for those of you who favour a more surreal technique you can always employ the following line, given to me by an artist friend. 'I say, do you realize that if this was where you lived, you would be home by now?'

Yes, *I'm* still trying to work that one out myself. I find it helps if you can sow a few seeds of doubt and insecurity into the minds of your late-night guests, and in this day and age nothing beats slipping this one in: 'Isn't it terrible how at this time of night, burglars make a beeline for houses where the owners are out enjoying themselves?'

You could mutter one or two additional lines about the shocking mess these criminals leave behind, but by the time you've finished speaking, they're usually half-way up their own garden path.

Now, you know me: I'm not a coarse person by any means. I wouldn't even associate with people like that. Just ask my PR adviser, Sir Les Patterson. I jealously guard my clean-cut image but there are times when a little honest vulgarity pays dividends with particularly thick-skinned guests.

To that end, at some stage in the proceedings, interrupt the conversation of the bore in question by painfully raising one buttock, grimacing pitifully and inquiring: 'Tell me, have you any experience of squeezing boils?'

Gross, I grant you, but the bottom line (if you'll pardon the pun) is that it is effective. Employed in the right manner, it will empty a room full of drunken sailors.

If your sensitivities baulk at such a ploy, you could always try raising the anxiety level. Try this little snail-shifter for size. Point to where they are sitting and say: 'Do you know, that's the very chair that his Lordship dropped dead in exactly twelve months ago to this very minute.' And if that doesn't do the trick, add: 'Would you like to inspect his ashes?' It's surprising how reluctant they are to take you up on the offer.

It is also amazing how desperate you can get. At a recent house party, in an attempt to rid myself of a person who just kept being there, I flung myself violently to the floor, coughed ear-splittingly until blue in the face and choked bravely: 'Don't worry. It isn't catching. Well, at least that's what they told me at the Hospital for Infectious Diseases.' The chap didn't even stay to say goodnight.

Subtle suggestion is a mainstay of my armoury. Why is it that when you talk about someone having nits, you simply have to scratch you head? See – you're doing it now. Well, we all know the lengths that people will go to avoid contact with those unwanted tiny visitors that our pets bring into the house from time to time. To play on this, start scratching like mad all over and grunt.

The dual-purpose rabid dog ruse: Guest deterrent and carpet shampoo all in one

If wit is your forte, you could essay an attempt at mild sarcasm such as: 'I'm glad you came to visit us. Your stay has considerably shortened the winter.'

It's also worth trying: 'On your way out, would you ask the milkman to leave six extra pints?' or even: 'Shall we all go outside to listen to the dawn chorus?'

If these little sallies go over their heads, offer to explain the terms of the Maastricht Treaty in great detail to them. Alternatively, if the visitor is of a sickly nature, try the following: 'Great news – Great-Aunt Flo's promised to come in and show us her cabaret regurgitation act.'

It may also help to try varying the stratagem. For instance, if it is the middle of summer, why not use a bit of subtlety and get the village choir to come and sing Christmas carols at the front door.

The options are endless. One of my all-time favourites is brilliant in its simplicity and apparent politeness. You rise slowly from your chair with great deliberation and murmur gently: 'Ahem, well well, just look at the time. Hope we haven't kept you up,' then slap your thigh, raise the eyes skyward and exclaim, 'Oh dear, silly me – this is *our* house, isn't it!' If the fish fail to bite on that one, you've no option but to walk menacingly towards them with your hair in plaits, wearing a ballet frock and saying: 'Would you like to see my Bonnie Langford impression?'

Of course, you could be *really* unlucky and be landed with some irksome pest on whom none of the above has any effect whatsoever. There is no need to get downhearted, however.

A sure-fire way of getting rid of an unwanted guest, and one that has never failed me on all the many occasions I have used it, is this. Simply adopt a sickly grin and say innocently, 'I say. Have you heard the latest Tony Blackburn jokes?' Stand well back or you'll get crushed in the stampede. And if *that* doesn't work, you are in trouble.

Well, time's getting on. What on earth are you hanging about here for? I've told you all I know. For goodness sake, have you nothing better to do? No? Well, I'll tell you what. Would you like to see my Crinkley Bottom holiday snaps? They're really interesting. I've got two

or three thousand here in this old plastic shopping
bag. I say . . . where are you going? Come back!
   Now THAT one works *every* time!

20. Bibliography

Noel Edmonds wishes to acknowledge the guidance and inspiration he received from the following publications in compiling this book:

Non-fatal Port Passing
Which Tablecloth?
Scotland's Finest Malt Whiskies, and Where to Hide Them
Three-Course Meals for Under a Fiver
Pick Up Your Fish Knife Without Social Ostracism
Flower Arranging the Inuit Eskimo Way
Conversation for One
Cummerbunds Without Tears
6,000 Excuses for Forgetting Your Wallet
The Short Man's Guide to Romance
Look Good in Gunny Sacks
The Gobi Nomads' Guide to Home Décor
Perfume by Mail Order
Take Another Look at Lapland Wines
The Mudman Spring Fashions Catalogue
The Anti-Servant Self-Defence Guide
Unpleasant Abdominal Disorders: Deflecting the Blame
Bad Neighbours – Instantly!

The Third Reich's Book of Practical Jokes

Nosebleeds, Trauma, and Multiple Fractures: A Legal Defence

You, Too, Can be a Borgia

1,001 Things to Do with Arsenic

A Song, a Dance, a Night in the Cells: A Leeds United Fans' Guide to Home Entertainment

The Marquis de Sade Game Book

The UK Register of Salmonella Bacteria Breeders

Home-Brew Anti-freeze – The Alibis

Teach Yourself World Population Control

Emergency Lawyers in the UK

Vegetarian Body Disposal

Geneva Convention on Human Rights: The Loopholes

Paperback Publishers in Great Britain – A Blackmailers' Guide